Seven Rivers to Churchill

Jim Lewis

ISBN: 1523393939
ISBN-13: 978-1523393930

Dedication

This book is dedicated to the one who has dedicated her life to me. She has been my best friend for nearly fifty years. She has been there in times of immense need and in times of incredible prosperity, beside me in times of sorrow and happiness. She laughs when I laugh and cries when I cry. We share the same deep faith, the same values in life and dream many of the same dreams. Her presence in my life provides me with an unending source of inspiration and encouragement. Thank you Sharron Lewis, my amazing wife, for all that you are and mean to me. This book is dedicated to you with all my love.

CONTENTS

Special Thanks

I thank God for the tests in life which have prepared me with strength and perseverance required in the planning and completion of this trip.

Thanks to Ed Damiani for agreeing to go with me and hanging in there from beginning to end; and to his bride, Kim, for her support of Ed and me throughout the trip.

A big thank you goes to Ric from Churchill River Canoe Outfitters, Andrea, Program Liaison Officer / Canadian Heritage Rivers Board Secretariat, Catherine from the Paddle Manitoba Club, and others including conservation officers and railroad employees who responded to my correspondence as I readied for the trip.

Much gratitude is extended to Chuck Newberg of Spring Creek Outfitters in Mt Iron, MN for his assistance in making this trip possible.

Thanks to Joan Bibeau and to Mike Rom for helping with logistics at the beginning of our adventure.

I also want to send a special thank you to Jerry Dunlop and his staff at Dunlop's Fly-in Fishing Lodge for their kindness and hospitality. And to all others along the way who assisted with helping hands and pointing us in the right direction, especially Donny Big George, Sam, Carl, Kevin, Chris, and Dennis.

Thank you to all the good friends and family who followed our route and cheered us on.

Great appreciation also goes out to our close friends, Cliff and Lois

Allen, who became such an important part of the journey as they accompanied Sharron on the train to Churchill to welcome us as we arrived.

Of course this work would not have been completed if it were not for those who spent hours reading and correcting draft manuscripts. Thank you to my wife, Sharron, our son, TJ, Ron and Wanda Ulseth, Harvey and Norma Frisco, and Bonnie Larson for a job well done.

Thanks to you the reader as well, blessings to you on all your adventures.

If I have missed anyone, I apologize. It was not intentional.

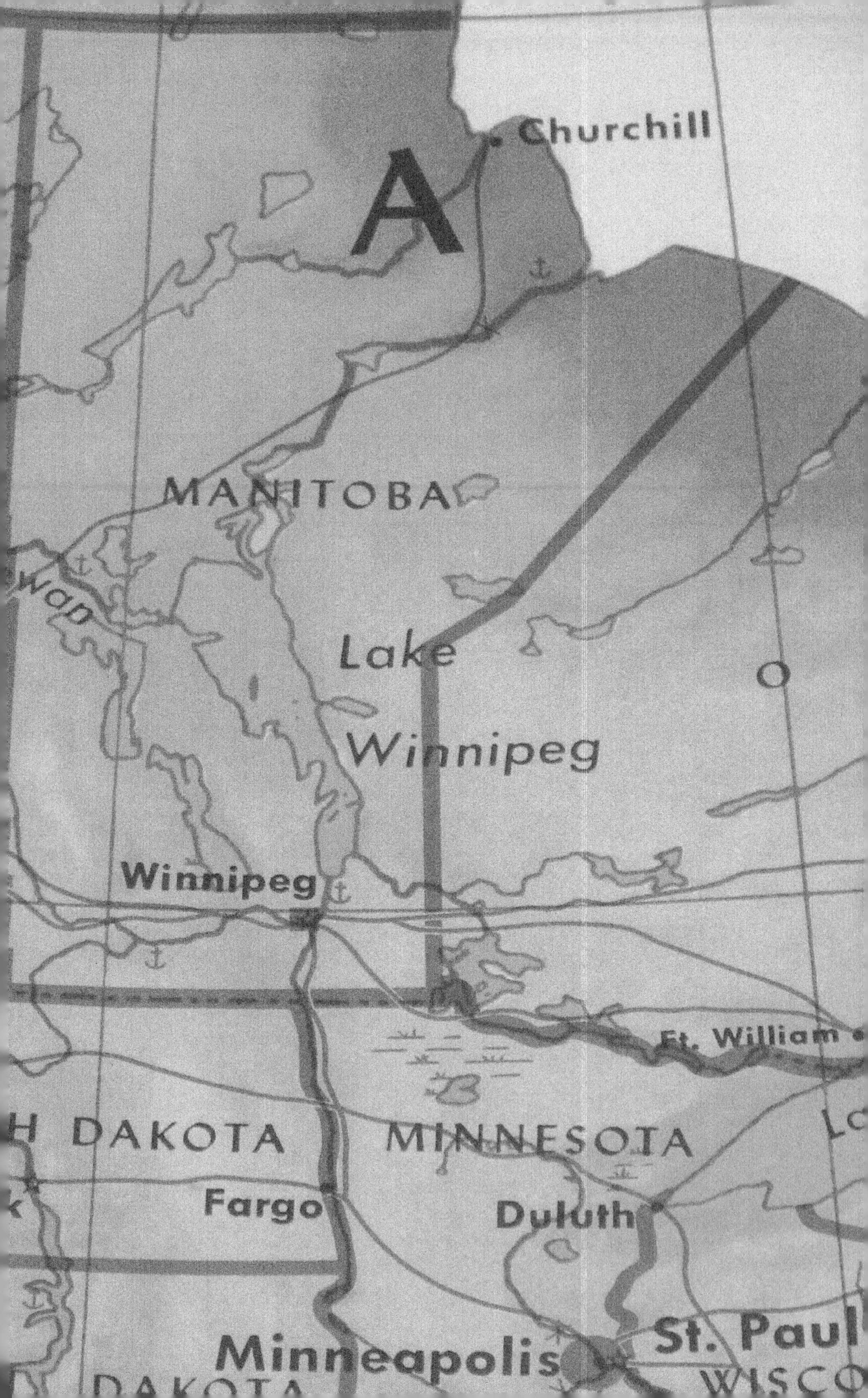

Churchill

A

MANITOBA

Lake

Winnipeg

O

Winnipeg

Ft. William

H DAKOTA

MINNESOTA

Fargo

Duluth

Minneapolis

St. Paul

DAKOTA

WISCO

Preface

When making my move towards retirement in 2007 my sister told me that she knew I would be good at it. My aim was to not disappoint her! To quote Robert F. Kennedy, "Only those who dare to fail greatly can ever achieve greatly."

Since then people have asked the question, "Have you always been this adventurous?" The fact is that my actual adventures pale deeply in comparison to the daydreams of my Walter Mitty mind. (My wife, Sharron, of nearly 48 years has told me that if you have to explain it, it's not worth it.) In this case though, I feel compelled to explain the character of Walter Mitty, created in a short story by James Thurber in 1939. The short story focuses on the escape from a mundane life through the vivid imagination of an easily distracted and unassuming little man who accompanies his wife on weekly shopping trips. Mitty's mind's eye sees himself as a pilot of a U.S. Navy flying-boat in a violent storm, then as a top notch surgeon performing an impossible operation, then as an imperturbable assassin testifying in court, then as a Royal Air Force pilot who does not hesitate to volunteer for an audacious, secret suicide mission to blow up an enemy ammunition dump. As for me, most of our friends see me as a blend between the Energizer Bunny and a half-crazed man who enjoys a walk on the wild side. I have to admit though, sometimes when my batteries begin to wear down, the old adage comes to mind, activity breeds energy. And the first activity that often comes to mind is "hammock" – I embrace the activity and rebound with energy.

Adventures are like potato chips, you can't stop after just one. I was blessed to retire at the wonderful age of 57, a little later than some, but a little earlier than most. I have also been blessed with Sharron, my wife, my friend, and all that makes me complete. She is willing to let me dream and supports me when I attempt to make those dreams come true. In the first five years of my retirement, I managed to complete a 2,300 mile kayak trip, from the Mississippi Headwaters at Lake Itasca, down the great river to one hundred miles beyond New Orleans to Mile Marker -0- in the Gulf of Mexico. I then wrote and published the book, "Ka-Ka-Ska-Ska" (Headwaters to the Gulf – in a kayak). As I sat with a friend on a dock in Venise, LA, the last road access on the Mississippi, waiting for Sharron to arrive with the car to take us back to northern Minnesota, I turned to him and said, "I think anyone who can paddle the Mississippi should be able to hike the Grand Canyon. It can't be that hard, can it? How far do you think it is across?"

My first crossing of the canyon, (twenty-three miles one way, with a 10,000 foot elevation change) was three days and two nights going rim-to-rim and back again with some of the same friends who accompanied me on the Mississippi. While in the area, we extended our stay as we logged in another forty-plus miles hiking in the slot canyons and the hills of Zion National Park and in Bryce Canyon National Park. That was in mid-May. The trip was so incredible that I convinced two of our three children to return in August of the same year. Sharron and I drove from Minnesota, picking up our son who lived in Nebraska and meeting our daughter in Las Vegas; she had flown up from Texas. The "kids" and I began at the North Rim, hiking down the North Kaibab Trail to Phantom Ranch then made our exit up the South Rim via the Bright Angel Trail on the same day. Sharron drove the car around to meet us. I told you she was supportive!

The next year, it was back to paddling, and a little bit of pedaling. I found a paddle partner willing to kayak to Churchill, Manitoba. Sharron took the two day train ride up from Winnipeg to meet us in Churchill. That same summer, my first Grand Canyon team and I bicycled the 1,100 miles around Lake Superior – twelve days.

Another year passed and it was time to go global! Sharron and I had been planning a trip to Africa, and early on in the process I asked what she thought of me climbing Mount Kilimanjaro as long as we were in the neighborhood. I was not too surprised at her response, "Go for it." Since returning from Africa, there has been another day hike across the Grand Canyon, more river trips (ranging from a weekend outing to 500 miles), bike trips, and camping getaways. Still there are more of those sorts of dreams on the drawing board. In between my outdoor adventures, Sharron and I have fit in two four-week-long road trips in our old Corvette and have also traveled to Europe, the Middle East, Hawaii, Alaska, Florida, New York and Washington D.C. plus thousands of miles in the car to visit our six grandchildren. Yeah, I guess I am pretty good at retirement…

"A man is not old until his regrets take the place of dreams"

Yiddish Proverb

THE RIVER

deep below the surface

deep where no light has ever shown

the source is unknown

its beginnings are hidden

gaining strength with each new day

as a dream that knows no boundaries

left to wander without control

its path determined by what it can consume

defying man's desire to conquer

seemingly nothing will slow its progress

emotions run high along the way

from comfort to fear and back again

those who have made the journey agree

the flow goes on and on to no real end.

Jim Lewis

(In honor of all who battle cancer)

SEVEN RIVERS TO CHURCHILL

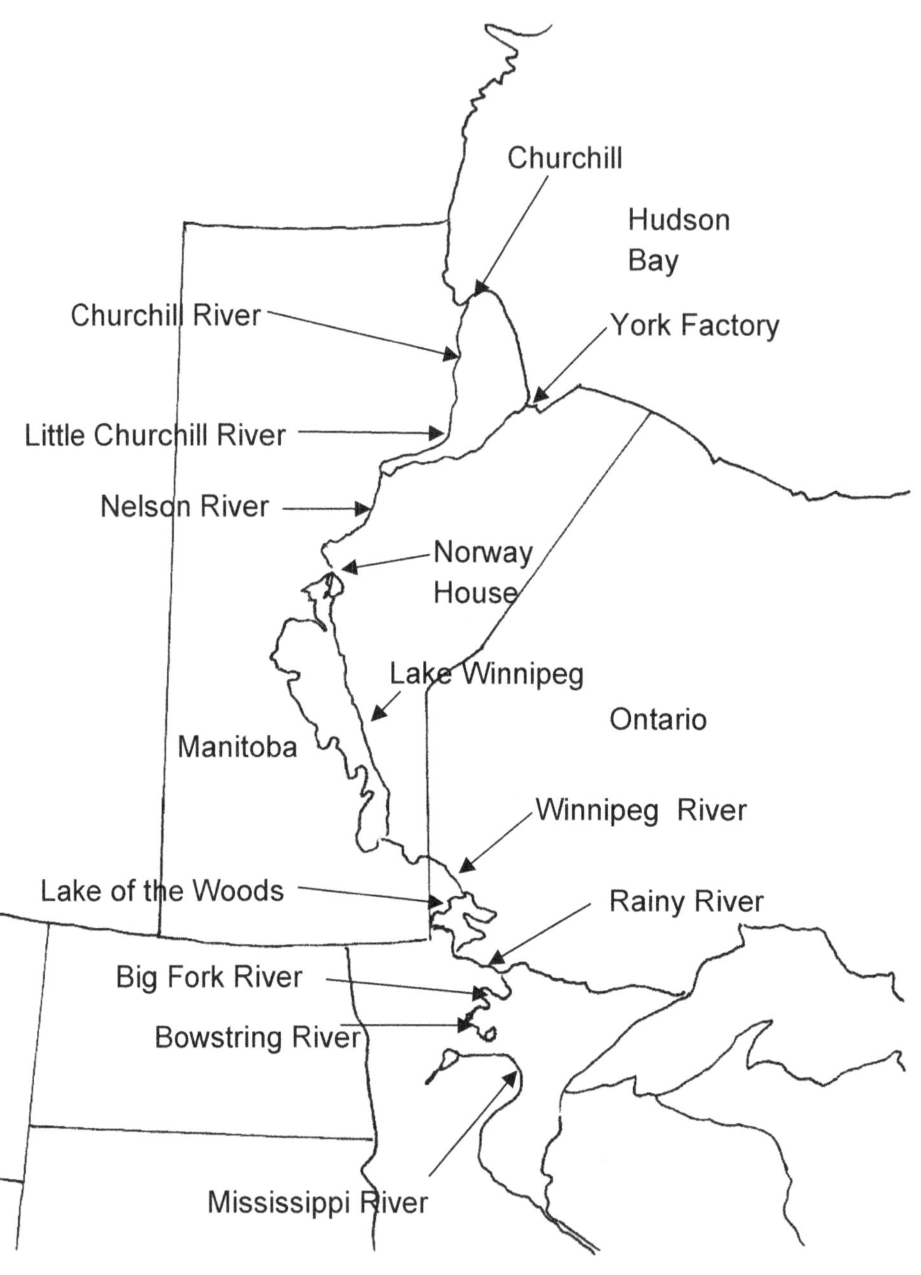
Churchill
Hudson
Bay
Churchill River
York Factory
Little Churchill River
Nelson River
Norway
House
Lake Winnipeg
Ontario
Manitoba
Winnipeg River
Lake of the Woods
Rainy River
Big Fork River
Bowstring River
Mississippi River

"I'm sure it can be done…"

In 2008 I completed a 2,300 mile kayak trip down the Mississippi from the Headwaters at Lake Itasca in Minnesota to Mile Marker -0-, 100 miles beyond New Orleans. In my mind, it only made sense for me to now go north to Hudson Bay. What doesn't make sense is that by definition the Gulf of Mexico is actually a bay and Hudson Bay, by definition is actually a gulf. Not that it makes any difference.

Looking at a map of the Mississippi Headwaters, it appears to take the shape of a giant "question mark" where the great river flows through Lake Winnibigoshish. At the crest of that question mark is where it brushes against the Laurentian Divide. North of the Laurentian Divide rivers and streams flow north; south of the Divide, they flow south – separating the watershed of the Atlantic Ocean from that of the Arctic Ocean. This is the perfect place to begin an adventure going north. Normal people, when planning a paddle trip to Hudson Bay choose the Eric Sevareid route on the Red River, (if actually there were normal people considering such a trip.)

First things first though, I had to find someone to accompany me. I sent an invitation to the members of the Itasca Kayakers. It went out to nearly a hundred email addresses. In response, a handful of people were willing to go as far as the U.S. / Canada border, but no one had the time or desire to take on a longer trip. I continued the search making my pitch to anyone I came across with a kayak. Finally, in midsummer 2009, while on a club outing with the Itasca Kayakers, our group crossed paths with another group paddling the same waters. Without any qualms, I put forth the best presentation I could to paddlers of the other group. Again it all seemed to be in vain, but I hoped the seed was planted. A few weeks passed and with a volley of emails to and from one of leaders in that group I had a taker!! I found someone who was willing to pursue a trip of a lifetime, at least through the planning stage.

My new partner, Ed, had recently gotten into kayaking after spending years paddling a canoe. Ed is former Navy, a submariner no less, who enjoys camping, hiking, mountain climbing, fishing and everything else out of doors. During his college years, Ed worked as a nightshift foreman at a facility where they made Gummi Bears. I'm not sure if the skill sets learned during this time would be of any use on the trip, but it did look good on his resume. The best part is that he teaches engineering at the local college, an educator with a month of free time during the summer and a taste for adventure. As it turns out, Ed happens to be the best topo-map reader I have ever met. It was a match made in heaven.

Then I began the daunting task of trying to connect as much of a water trail as possible between the Mississippi Headwaters and Hudson Bay, a route that could be accomplished in one month's time. After spending what seemed to be hundreds of hours searching hard copy and electronic topographical maps of Ontario and Manitoba, sending dozens of emails and making countless phone calls to lodge owners, wilderness outfitters, conservation officers, air charter services, and Rail Canada I finally found that it was possible to make it all the way to Churchill, MB within our time constraints. However, the route was not entirely by water – more on that later. Due to the difficulty of the route and likelihood of low water conditions on the lower Churchill River, ending a paddle trip in Churchill is not a very popular destination.

"Only those who dare to fail greatly
can ever achieve greatly."
Robert F. Kennedy

The Red River, aka Red River of the North, originates at the confluence of the Bois de Sioux and Otter Tail rivers between Minnesota and North Dakota. It flows north through the Red River Valley, forming the border of Minnesota and North Dakota and continuing into Manitoba, Canada. It empties into Lake Winnipeg, whose waters join the Nelson River and ultimately flows into Hudson Bay, which is considered part of the Arctic Ocean. Sevareid made this route popular in his book, Canoeing with the Cree; the tale of the canoe trip he took in 1930 with his pal Walter C. Port. The complete route took the pair up the Minnesota River from Minneapolis to its tributary the Little Minnesota River to Browns Valley. Sevareid and Port portaged to Lake Traverse and descended the Bois des Sioux River to the Red River of the North, which led to Lake Winnipeg, finally paddling down the Nelson River, Gods River, and Hayes River to York Factory on Hudson Bay.

It's understandable why people would select this course. It is well traveled. Therefore a lot of information is available describing the waterway and locations of the portages, etc. This is not to say it is easy; the trip still requires a great deal of planning and skill to make it successfully. At first, we too gave consideration to taking the Sevareid route. One problem with this route was the Red River. From what I could find out, it was not much more than a long muddy ditch with little opportunity to see over its banks. The second concern was the expense of the egress from York Factory. There are no roads to or from York Factory, leaving only four "reasonable" options for a way home:

1) Continue to paddle out into Hudson Bay approximately 87.8 miles then turn southeast to follow the shoreline, but not too close because of the twenty or so miles of mud flats which occur as the tide recedes. Then paddle a mere 377 miles before making another course correction to the south beyond Akimiski Island in James Bay. Once the Island is in the rearview mirror, make a hard right and don't stop until you reach land. Here you will need to make a 349 mile portage to Lake Superior. Upon entering the big lake, paddle 300 plus/minus miles in a westerly direction to the city of Duluth where you can call a friend for a ride.

2) Turn around and paddle back home the same way you came. Remember it's all upstream.

3) This option sends the needle on the *Does-This-Seem-Practical* meter a little more to the right, but not yet in the green. Once you reach the fort at York Factory, pack up your gear and take a short five mile portage across the bog to the Nelson River. Put in and paddle upstream to the village of Sundance where you can catch the train to Winnipeg. From there, you should be able to arrange for a ride home with a friend. According to what I read, the problem with this plan is not the portage across the bog. That is in all probability doable. Paddling fifty miles upstream on most rivers is not a big deal either, however, the dam at Gillam located beyond Sundance could present a bit of a problem. This is not your ordinary dam. It is gargantuan, the biggest hydro dam on the Nelson, and when it opens it creates an extremely powerful flow downstream. Now put yourself in a kayak heading upstream and the dam opens unexpectedly while you are negotiating the tidal flow (coming in or going out – your choice).

4) The most popular option is to have an airplane pick you up and fly you over to Gillam where you can hop the train to Winnipeg and figure it out from there. The flight services I checked had planes capable of carrying only two passengers, one kayak or one canoe, plus typical gear. The cost was $1,700 per flight, seventy-five miles one way. We had no interest in paddling a canoe for any distance, much less hundreds of miles across country, especially if guns were on board. So our way out of York Factory would mean the cost of two flights. Of course we could sacrifice one of our kayaks to the locals. Not a bad plan, but not real palatable either.

And that is how I, with incredible wisdom (or, lack thereof), decided to pursue the "road less traveled" -- a *road* that I spent countless hours studying topographical maps with a magnifying glass trying to pick a route through Canada from one waterway to the next, finding traces of what appeared to be portages. But then again, those faint little dots in a row could also represent snow mobile trails across frozen swamp intended for winter use only. It was a process similar to working your way through a maze, success for awhile, then dead end, backtrack, and try again in a new direction. I also searched the internet in hope of connecting with lodge owners, outfitters, or whoever may have a clue how to connect all the dots. Most said, "I'm sure it can be done, but I don't think that is a very good idea." Some sample responses…

An outfitter in Saskatchewan:

Hi Jim,

There seems to be very little information on that trip. Very few people now paddle that portion of the Churchill. I have no recent information on that portion of the Churchill River. Because much of the Churchill River water is diverted to run the generator turbines on the Nelson River, the Churchill from the dam at the downstream end of Southern Indian Lake to Hudson Bay often has very little water in it. Many who are paddling this route will go over the divide from the Churchill to the Seal River and paddle that river instead. It is a much more interesting river. The route between the rivers goes from Granville Lake into Barrington Lake to Big Sandy Lake on the Seal R. *I've got more detail on that route if you like. And I do have a fair bit of information on the Seal River. I'm sorry I can't help you more.*

Sincerely,
Ric
Churchill River Canoe OutfittersForest House Wilderness Lodge

....

I found the route on my map that Ric described, roughly 550 miles with one opportunity for resupplying along the way. That didn't bother me, so I thought I would dig deeper.

From the Heritage River website (Note that this information is regarding the last half of the trek only):

Of the four major rivers in northern Manitoba, the Seal River alone remains completely undeveloped, wild and rugged. In contrast to the impoundments on the Churchill and the Nelson, and the rich fur trade and exploration history of the Hayes, the Seal River shows virtually no evidence of modern human activity. Although in the days before written history the river flowed through a major native hunting and fishing ground, the Seal now attracts only a few native people and small groups of hardy wilderness adventurers.

For these groups, travel downriver may require two to four weeks of difficult yet exhilarating boating. First, an extensive cold-water lake is encountered where winds can create dangerous waves; then, numerous long rapids in a totally isolated, sub-arctic environment test their survival skills; finally, travelers must navigate a boulder-strewn tidal estuary.

The Seal River is located in the roadless wilderness of northern Manitoba, 1000 km by air charter from Winnipeg. The Seal estuary is 45 km across Hudson Bay from Churchill. Other than Churchill (population 1,300), the only settlement in the area is Tadoule (population 250), a small Chipewyan community located along the South Seal River at Tadoule Lake.

The Seal begins its course at Shethanei Lake ringed by the magnificent sand-crowned eskers that are so much a part of the Seal River landscape. Then, passing stands of black spruce, its velocity increases toward the Big Spruce River Delta, and accelerates dramatically into the rapids and gorges which surround Great Island. Beyond the island, the river leaves the boreal forest and enters a sparsely-treed, transitional subarctic environment of tundra and heath, christened by the natives the "Land of Little Sticks". Finally the Seal flows through barren arctic tundra, huge boulder fields and complex rapids, spilling into a beautiful estuary where its freshwaters mix with the salt of Hudson Bay.

Except for the less than two dozen skilled rafting and canoeing parties which visit the river each year, and the occasional native fisherman and trapper, there is virtually no human activity along the Seal River. The remote, roadless nature of this region has meant that activities such as mining exploration have been costly, air-supported ventures, and even the discussion stages of any development of the area's hydro potential are many years away.

....

After reading the above and discovering that the thirty-five miles from the mouth of the Seal to Churchill cannot be paddled – leaving us to either find a water taxi or floatplane – I removed the option of a route including the Seal River from our list of possibilities.

A response received from the secretary of the Canadian Heritage River Board:

Hello Mr. Lewis,

I do not actually know if that section of the river is accessible or advisable for a canoe trip and my best suggestion is to contact Ken Schykulski with Manitoba Conservation kschykulsk@gov.mb.ca. *He is the Planner for Canadian Heritage Rivers in that province and is an avid canoeist.*

The Churchill River has in fact been nominated as a Canadian Heritage River, but it is only nominated on the Saskatchewan side.

My other suggestions for you to help plan this exciting canoe trip: Try looking at Canoeing route books written for each province such as Hap Wilson book on Canoe Routes in Manitoba. Get in touch with the Manitoba Chapter of the Canadian Recreational Canoeing Association-- (now called Paddle Canada). Ask if they can help get you in contact with people and route descriptions. Post a question on "My Canadian Canoe Routes": http://www.myccr.com/ *asking about the route.*

Get topographic maps. http://ess.nrcan.gc.ca/mapcar/top_e.php

Of course, there are many other books and resources out there to help you plan a long trip such as this -- again, posting on the Forum of the Canadian Canoe

Routes website will help steer you towards those others have found most useful.
http://www.myccr.com/SectionForums/index.php.

Best of luck,
Andrea
Program Liaison Officer / Agent de liaison du programme
Canadian Heritage Rivers Board Secretariat /
Secrétariat de la Commission des rivières du patrimoine canadien
Parks Canada / Parcs Canada

....

I emailed Ken S (as mentioned above), but never received a response.

From Paddle Manitoba (a club located in Winnipeg):

Hello Jim,

Off the top of my head, I am not aware of information about the Churchill River, but I will do some digging with some of my kayaking contacts and see what we come up with.

Catherine
Paddle Manitoba

....

Again, no further correspondence from Paddle Manitoba is ever received.

Cour'age (ker'ij) n. 1, lack of fear; bravery. 2, to be dim-witted

The vision of a kayak trip to Churchill was beginning to look more like a pipedream to nowhere. Well, maybe for someone else, but it's not my style to give up so easily. I recall a comment made by a supervisor on my annual performance review, back when I was in the work world. "With Jim, everything is possible -- the impossible just takes longer." It was time to take on the impossible and make it happen. Perhaps this whole thing should not have been labeled impossible, but just a little more challenging than most people would find comfortable.

After what seemed to be an overwhelming task at times, I at last settled on the best option for a path forward:

- Follow Bowstring River from Bowstring Lake (located a little more than six miles from Lake Winnibigoshish) to Dora Lake, the source of the Big Fork River. The Bowstring River connects four lakes: Bowstring Lake to Sand Lake to Little Sand Lake to Rice Lake to Dora Lake, a distance of twenty-two miles.
- Paddle the Big Fork River to the confluence of the Rainy River at the Canada Border, 160 miles.
- Enter the Rainy River and follow the Minnesota / Canada border to Lake of the Woods, 65 miles.
- Continue north across Lake of the Woods to Kenora, Ontario, 85 miles.
- Paddle down the Winnipeg River to Lake Winnipeg, 150 miles.
- Head north across Lake Winnipeg to Norway House, MB, 275 miles.
- Continuing on from Norway House, paddle north on the Nelson River through Sipiwesk Lake to a portage to Sabomin Lake to Landing Lake, exiting at Thicket Portage, Manitoba, 185 river miles from Norway House.
- Catch the train in Thicket Portage to Thompson, Manitoba, 30 miles. Timing is essential. The train stops every two days.
- Charter a plane equipped with floats (must be a de Havilland Otter or similar, able to transport two kayaks) to Campbell Lake, 60 miles.

- Paddle east on Campbell Lake to Pelletier Lake to Waskaiowaka Lake and the exit point of the Little Churchill River, 40 miles.
- Paddle northeast on the Little Churchill River to the confluence of the Churchill River.
- Follow the Churchill River to Hudson Bay. It is roughly 220 river miles from Campbell Lake to Churchill. (Arrangements were made for my wife, Sharron, and our friends, Cliff and Lois, to take the train from Winnipeg, Manitoba to Churchill to meet us for the two-day return ride on the rails back to Winnipeg.)

Ed Damiani and Jim Lewis, author

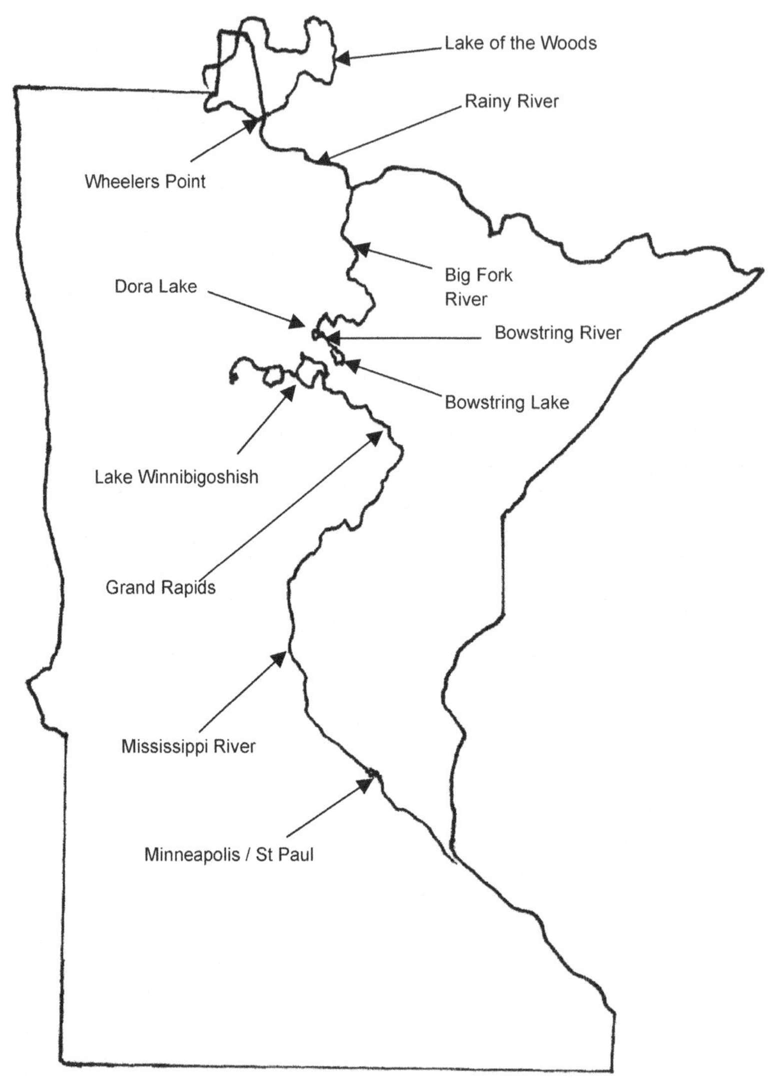
Lake of the Woods
Rainy River
Wheelers Point
Big Fork
River
Dora Lake
Bowstring River
Bowstring Lake
Lake Winnibigoshish
Grand Rapids
Mississippi River
Minneapolis / St Paul

Minnesota

Our trip to Churchill was completed in three separate sections. The first section was a twenty-two mile day trip from Bowstring Lake to Dora Lake. In my research I had discovered there were two miles of this particular stretch of river that grows over quickly in the spring, making it extremely difficult to negotiate with any watercraft. A friend of mine did a flyover in mid-April to check it out. "You may have another week at the most to make it." I went the next day, knowing I'd rather paddle through the channel than attempt it later risking having to wade through who knows how many centuries of droppings left behind by migratory birds.

A month later on a dreary Monday morning my paddle partner, Ed, and I launched our kayaks from the boat landing on the west side of Dora Lake in northern Itasca County. As we eased through the bulrushes that were growing in the shallows, a heavy fog rose to meet the rain-threatening gray sky overhead. The only bright spot of the morning was Ed's wife, Kim, who delivered us to our beginning. We packed our gear, took some photos of each other, and then with long determined strokes we started off against a light chop on the water's surface toward the Big Fork River exiting on the far north shore. The Big Fork would take us to the Rainy River along the international border, then onto Lake of the Woods. We were planning to spend no more than five days on this section. Ed's daughter was graduating from high school so it was imperative for him to get back home to take care of important family obligations. A short trip was a good opportunity to see how the two of us worked together as well as providing a chance to discuss our plans in greater detail. Up till now most of our communication had been done via email. Besides, Ed and I had only paddled together for a few hours one day.

A light but steady rain began soon after we launched. Loons, ducks, and trumpeter swans cheered us on our way. We paddled throughout the day on good flow, making it thirty-one miles down river to the town of Big Fork late in the afternoon. Taking breaks into consideration, our overall average speed for the day was slightly less than four miles per hour. There was no reason to think we couldn't make it to the designated DNR Busticogan Campsite another fifteen miles downstream before dark. That's what you would think anyway – doing the math. Most investment management companies tell you in the fine print, "Past performance is not a reliable indicator of future performance." The same holds true for trekking of any sort, whether on water or land. The campsite we had our sights on was located a mile beyond the bridge that crosses Minnesota Highway 1. We were still a mile upstream from the bridge when the sun went from dim to useless. Heavy cloud cover was a guarantee to eliminate any benefit of the yet-to-rise full moon.

The map revealed a Class I boulder-bed rapids in the flow beneath the bridge. (Class I is defined as "easy rapids with small waves and few obstructions." Class II is "a set of rapids with waves up to three feet high. Some maneuvering is required." Interesting how the ratings go from "small waves" in a Class I to "waves up to three feet" in a Class II.) Wouldn't you think if the waves were, say two feet, the map would give a warning of Class I.5 rapids?

Neither Ed nor I considered scouting the rapids. Dark as it was, it would have been an exercise in futility anyway. Nor did we attempt an exit upstream to portage around the bridge, ahead of the grumblings of river against the rocks. That would have made way too much sense. Instead, the anxiety we had was cast aside. I took a deep breath, exhaled a silent prayer, and entered the trough like I knew what was I was doing. It became quite obvious all too soon – no clue. Above the turbulence of the rushing water, we both call out.

"Rock,"

"Rock,"

"Another rock,"

"Oh, here's another one."

The promise I had made Sharron (like on any other trip) that I would be careful rang loudly in my ears, "*I'll take it easy and go slow.*" Suddenly I found my kayak crosswise in the current resting at a precarious angle on the upstream side of one of hundreds of boulders. I imagined it to be the size of a "smart car" submerged below the surface like an iceberg. Briefly, very briefly, I considered spending the night in the cockpit and perhaps work on a solution at first light. Then primal instinct kicked in. I commenced bouncing, thrusting, and rocking, as if I was demonstrating the greatest and latest craze in sit-down cardio vascular workout equipment for an after-midnight infomercial. As my heart was reaching the target rate, my kayak was dislodged by the force of the river, spun around in the darkness, and once again pointed in a direction I believed to be downstream.

The dim shadows of the tree tops were just one shade lighter than the overcast night sky. On river-right, there appeared to be a break in the trees. I recalled that the map had indicated a boat landing. I paddled hard. Ed did the same. On the shore, we discussed our options, camp there at the landing or chance finding the designated site another mile downstream. It was unanimous: stay, even though camping at a boat landing is one of my least favorite things to do. I've said it before and I'll say it again, you never know who might show up in the middle of the night. There was an empty school van parked near a trailhead leading from the parking area. The kayaks were dragged down the trail leaving enough real estate between them and the van for our two tents.

We considered the day a success. We paddled forty-eight miles, most of it in the rain, but stayed relatively comfortable. We endured against a mild headwind and negotiated a set of rapids we could not see. And now, we had been given a place to rest, less than ten yards from a sign stating, "NO OVERNIGHT CAMPING."

"If we confess our sins,
He is faithful and just to forgive us..."
1 John 1:9

Before this region was settled by the Europeans 250 years ago, this was where the Woodland Culture Indians made their home. One of the most notable groups was the Laurel. The Laurel built Grand Mound, a burial hill located near the mouth of the Big Fork, forty feet high and more than a hundred feet across. The Laurel gave way to the Blackduck, who may have been the direct predecessors of the Dakota. The Dakota, or Sioux, inhabited the region until the Ojibwe laid claim to the area.

At the turn of the century, millions of board feet of pine logs were floated down the Big Fork River to lumber mills in Ontario. It flows freely one hundred sixty-eight miles through wild and scenic state forestland, including Big Fork State Forest, Pine Island State Forest,

George Washington State Forest, Koochiching State Forest, and the Chippewa National Forest. The river's waters flow north through the watershed that goes to Hudson Bay, following the Rainy River across southern Ontario, onto Lake Winnipeg, then into the Nelson River in Manitoba. The Big Fork is among the few rivers in northern Minnesota that is part of that watershed. Much of the watershed was once covered by glacial Lake Agassiz.

Most of the Big Fork River is easy to paddle with several areas of Class I rapids. There are two spectacular water falls that need to be portaged; Little American Falls (Class III-IV) and Big Falls (Class IV-VI). Stream flow generally peaks in late April and falls during the summer, when some of the rapids may be impassable. The low-lying Big Fork valley is pastoral in places and in other parts wild. Scattered small farms break up a forest of pine, spruce, fir, cedar, aspen and birch. River travelers encounter only two small towns along the way; Big Fork and Big Falls.

Generally, wildlife in this area is abundant including timber wolves, bobcats, lynx, beavers, and otters – although on our paddle, all these creatures proved to be quite shy except for the beavers. Of the big game mix, you can generally count on seeing moose, black bears, and white-tailed deer. Only the moose eluded us. We encountered literally hundreds of birds along the river, several species of ducks, osprey, bald eagles, and a variety of song birds.

"The rivers are our brothers. They quench our thirst.
The rivers carry our canoes, and feed our children.
If we sell you our land, you must remember,
and teach your children,
that the rivers are our brothers and yours,
and you must henceforth give the rivers
the kindness you would give any brother."
Chief Seattle - 1854

We woke from a good night's rest on the trail where we camped behind the school van, ate a hasty bowl of oatmeal, and set sail under blue skies. Pushing off from shore, our breath condensed in the cool air creating slight clouds that dispersed as quickly as the next one formed. As the sun rose above the tree line, the chill gave way to warmth and comfort.

One hour lapsed into two and two into three and then this day was gone as well, leaving only memories behind. Memories of fast water, and our victory of shooting through Powells Rapids, Muldoon Rapids and one other, not worthy of being named. However, when we arrived at American Falls we opted to deploy a measure of common sense and made our first portage. It was a perfect day on a pristine river as it wandered its way through a northern wilderness.

We'd gone fifty-six miles on that perfect day before tying off to the dock at Johnson's Landing, a MN DNR maintained campsite. Johnson's Landing has nearly an acre of mowed grass at a slight elevation above the river, an artesian well producing an endless supply of fresh spring water, and of course it was well stocked with blood thirsty mosquitoes. On the downside, this site had an access road off the nearby county highway. A small self-contained camper was set up overlooking the river. No one was around but it appeared that whoever it belonged to had been there awhile and was not intending to move soon. It didn't feel right, but the only other option for camping was over twenty miles away, impossible to make in the hour of daylight remaining. We secured our kayaks with a cable lock and set our tents up far away from the camper, near the edge of the mowing. Just about the time I was dozing off, I heard a vehicle approaching, rattling and squeaking over the potholes in the gravel road. I lay there "waiting for the other shoe to fall." The car stopped near the camper, the doors opened, and the first voice I heard was that of a female. For me that was good news; our neighbors were a couple, not some beer drinking yahoos out looking for trouble. Sleep came quickly and it lasted all night.

The neighbors had shown us respect, having been quiet. We returned the favor in the early morning hours, stealing away into a new day looking forward to whatever it was around the next bend. We reached the city of Big Falls after fifteen miles of beautiful but uneventful river. Visitors never ask how it got its name. The portage looked tough, through a city park, across the highway, and down through a campground on the bottom side of the falls. While I dragged the kayaks out of the water, Ed went off to do some negotiating with a city maintenance crew, who happened to have a pickup truck. It must have been an easy sell because Ed returned in a few minutes with his new friends and their truck. A difficult portage made easy; back on the water in no time!

The next stop was the mouth of the Big Fork at the confluence with the Rainy River, sixty-six miles from where we had camped at Johnson's Landing. But the day wasn't over yet even though the sun was making silhouettes of the trees to the west when we arrived. A DNR guide book I had read stated that a paddler should plan on ten to sixteen days to complete the entire Big Fork River. It took Ed and me three days. The two inches of rainfall on our first day set us up to make good time on good water. With the sun setting, it was one more of those end-of-the-day moments when you wonder if you haven't already let the last campsite slip away.

We continued a mile downstream on the Rainy River in fading light before spotting what appeared to be a flat sand point. Excellent! This should be a good place to spend the night. No such luck. The sand was not sand at all, it was a soft muck. Another hour passed with another three miles and still nothing even close to resembling a place to pitch a tent on the U.S. side. The later it got, the colder it got under the late-May clear sky. No doubt about it, there was a direct correlation between the dark and cold, and our being tired and anxious. In order to set foot on the Canada side, we would have to have had a Remote Area Border Crossing Permit. Even if we had, the permit can only be used in designated areas such as the Boundary Waters and Quetico Provincial Park – not here. Without regard for the useless permit we opted to risk a life of imprisonment. Ed and I paddled across to the foreign soil to find nothing but steep banks and too much undergrowth.

Over on the U.S side again, paddling along in the moonlit night, I lost track of how many times we stopped to check out a particular inviting site only to find it completely worthless; high grass, rocks, underbrush, no spot on the ground big enough for one tent, let alone two. What happened to the campsites the voyageurs used along this route so long ago? In desperation, we broadened our search beyond the immediate shoreline to what looked like pasture land on a high bank. Unfortunately there was not a good place to pull the kayaks up on shore, so it was a matter of balancing between rocks and mud to make a tie-off to the underbrush. On shore we found the riverbank much steeper than it had been in our mind's eye, and no easy access to whatever was up above. It was too late to be choosy. Up we went with our tents and sleeping bags in hand. On the summit we found a plowed field bordered with a wide flat ribbon of mowed grass. What the heck, we were now what gamblers refer to as being "pot committed." Too late to do anything else, the decision was made. It was 1:30 a.m. when we made the final step onto shore after covering a long seventy-six miles. Our tents were set up, one on each side of a lone fencepost positioned there for no other reason than to support a brand new *NO TRESPASSNG* sign. We weren't going to be there that long anyway. My light-weight sleeping bag was no competition against the overnight low of 40F. Our rest was completed four hours after we had landed. It was time to hit the trail again.

"I will refresh the weary
and satisfy the faint."
Jeremiah 31:25

The Rainy River flows east to west defining a relatively small portion of the U.S. border between Minnesota and Ontario, Canada. The waterway runs eighty miles through mature forests and rich farmland connecting Rainy Lake on the east to Lake of the Woods on the west. Centuries ago this river was a major route used by the voyageurs for transporting commerce. The Ontario side of the valley is known as the *Food Box of the North.* Major industries harvest the forests on the Minnesota side to produce a variety of wood related products ranging from paper to oriented strand board to custom cabinetry. The Rainy is home to walleye, northern pike, smallmouth bass, sturgeon and muskellunge. On land, visitors will find bear, deer, beaver, otter, eagles, and 200 other species of birds during migration.

Ed and I skipped breakfast, eager to get started again. Going down the steep bank wasn't any easier than coming up the night before. Not wanting to make more than one trip, our arms were loaded heavily with camping crap, the rocks were slippery with dew, and the undergrowth was even thicker than we had imagined it was in the dark. Each step was slow and deliberate. On the river's edge we liberated the boats from the scrub willows while balancing the hulls on the natural riprap near water's edge. It's hard enough to stow all that is required on a river excursion into a kayak when the boat is resting on a beach. Imagine how much more difficult it is when your fingers are cold and stiff as sausage links, while balancing the boat and yourself on slippery rocks, round and smooth. I doubt that the voyageurs complained, so I didn't either.

I have always claimed a small portion of my heritage to be French Canadian, perhaps a justification for my adventurous spirit. However, let me make it perfectly clear I am in no way to be compared to those fur trading canoeists – the voyageur, a French word which literally means "traveler". The voyageurs were contract employees hired by the fur trading companies to transport furs and trade goods from the 1690s until the 1850s. It was expected that each voyageur work fourteen to sixteen hours a day, paddle fifty strokes per minute and be able to carry two ninety pound bales at the same time across each portage. It probably goes without saying that the number one cause of death for a voyageur was complications from hernias. The second leading cause was drowning. Survivors of their contracts were quite often given the opportunity to suffer from broken limbs, twisted spines, and rheumatism. Working conditions included clouds of black flies and mosquitoes against which the best repellent was a mix of bear grease and skunk urine. The voyageur's daily schedule was deplorable in today's standards and probably was back then as well. He spent up to eight weeks on the trail at a time, waking each day as early as 3:00 a.m., and working five hours before having breakfast – in route. A couple hours past noon, lunch would be offered up. Lunch consisted of a chunk of jerky or maybe a biscuit to be consumed while they continued to paddle the thirty-six-foot-long canoes. At day's end, the canoes were emptied and flipped upside down to serve as shelters.

"I ask not for a lighter burden,
but for broader shoulders."
Jewish Proverb

Okay perhaps the voyageurs did complain, but I didn't. The day was worthy of nothing but praise; a postcard-perfect blue sky with a late-spring sun shining bright, edging up over the horizon to guarantee warmth in an hour, maybe two. The day played out like a dream with good weather, good company, and good flow. We were able to locate the elusive cell phone signal sometime in the middle of the afternoon and made final arrangements to rendezvous with my nephew, Mike. He had picked up my vehicle earlier in the week in order to help us with logistics on this leg of the trip.

We may never know how we could have been so wrong in our calculations, but showing up more than an hour and a half late caused a little anxiety for Mike. Unfortunately we had no way of contacting him to put his mind at ease. Hours before, we'd lost access to cell phone coverage almost as fast as we had found it. Mike waited for at least an hour after dark had settled in before finding a phone to call Sharron to ask if it was typical for me to be on the water so late.

"Oh yeah, don't worry. Sit tight and he'll show up." More times than not she's right, and sure enough she was right this time too. A few minutes after Mike's call, we were there.

We had reached Wheelers Point on the south side of Lake of the Woods putting a total of 236 miles behind us in the first four days of our journey. This was not a record by any standard but certainly an excellent start for our 1,220 mile paddle adventure across the wilds of Canada to the Polar Bear Capital of the World, Churchill, Manitoba.

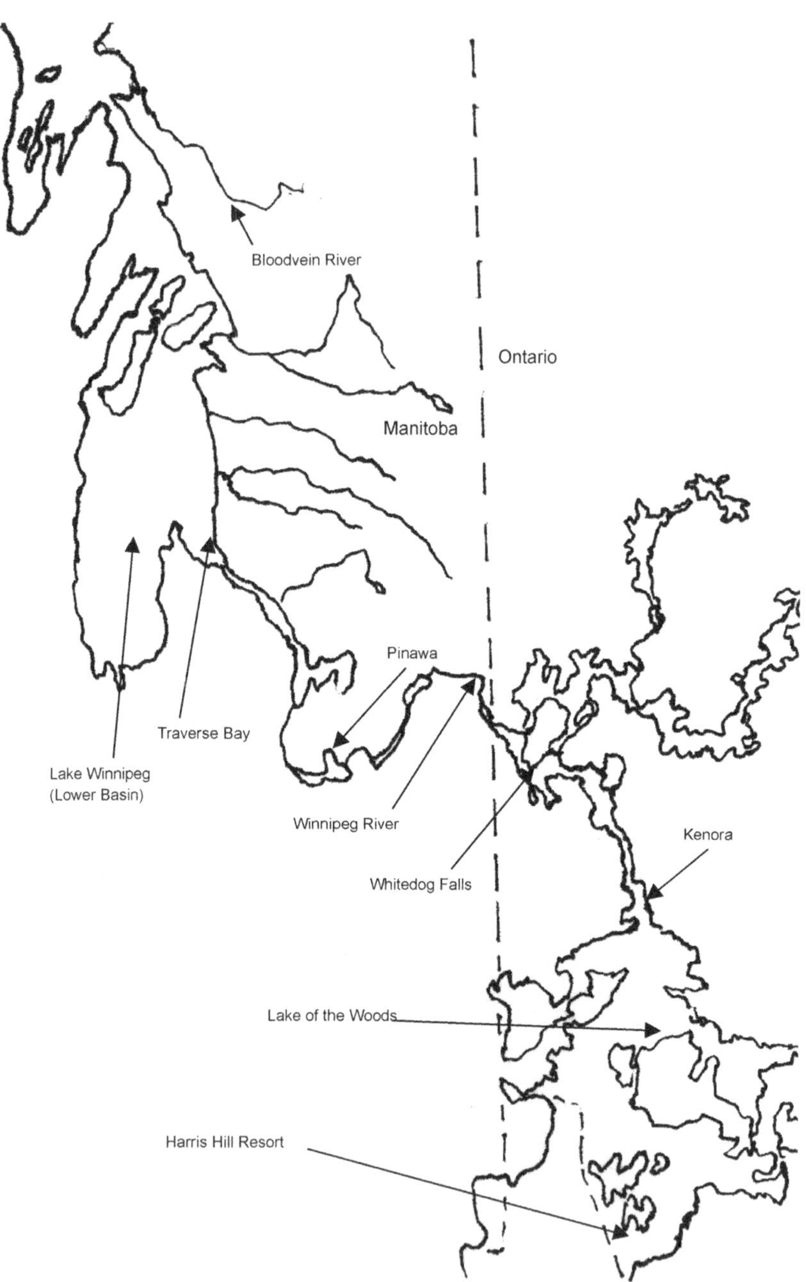
Bloodvein River
Ontario
Manitoba
Pinawa
Traverse Bay
Lake Winnipeg
(Lower Basin)
Winnipeg River
Kenora
Whitedog Falls
Lake of the Woods
Harris Hill Resort

Lake of the Woods to the Bloodvein

Ed's daughter graduated and he was able to get in a two-day camping trip with his sons in the BWCA. I managed to get a little yard work done. Together we did some fine tuning on our pack list and we put the kayaks back in Lake of the Woods after a six day break. Our mutual friend, Joan, assisted with logistics this time.

Crossing the border was interesting, taking more time than we had planned. We should have expected a delay because we were carrying weapons. I had asked everyone I was in contact with while planning the trip about the need of bringing a weapon along as personal protection against wildlife, bears in particular. The answer was always the same, "Yes." It was not what I was looking for, I like to travel light. Dragging a firearm along is not my idea of traveling light. The last person I asked about bringing a gun was a conservation officer assigned to northern Manitoba. I thought for sure that when I asked the "law," I would get the answer I was looking for. No such luck.

"Jim, I don't want you up here with anything less than a 30.06 rifle or a 12 gauge shotgun with slugs." It was settled then, bring guns. I wanted something compact that I could keep in the cockpit between the seat and hull. The answer, a Mossberg 500 pump action; an eighteen and a half inch barrel, pistol grip, synthetic stock, five and a half pounds, and an overall length less than twenty-nine inches. Still it was legal as a "long gun" and fit the criteria for a permit to take it across the border. I purchased it new, just for the trip. It was a nice gun and looked more than intimidating with its heat shield and ventilated rib, though I doubt any wildlife would give a hoot what it looked like.

At the crossing, the agent approached our vehicle and asked, "Purpose for wanting to enter Canada?"

"We want to kayak to Churchill."

She gazed without blinking, long and hard, shifting her eyes from Joan, to Ed, to me. Then with a very serious and puzzled look on her face, the agent asked, "Why?"

Good question. Unfortunately, we didn't have a good answer. It didn't seem to matter. We were given the green light. But then we informed the customs agent we had weapons and permits requiring final approval. "Pull around the back side of the building and park."

Another agent appeared a few minutes later to ensure the information on our permits matched what we were carrying. Ed didn't want to have to buy a new gun, so he brought his Winchester .30-30. It wasn't big enough according to the conservation officer I had spoken with, but we figured it was big enough to back up the 12 gauge. The customs agent gave Ed the oky-doky without any fanfare. The process didn't go quite as quickly for me. He took one look at what gave the appearance of a sawed off shotgun and said, "Lay it down right there and don't move! I'll be back."

He disappeared inside, not showing up again for several minutes. He brought a notepad, a pencil and a tape measure back with him. All the specs were recorded, checked and checked again. Then he took my permit and his little notepad back inside. Time passed, slowly. Finally he returned, handed my permit back to me and said everything was in order. We were free to go, but first… one question. "Where did you get that? That is one sweet little gun! I may have to get me one."

Our put-in was at Harris Hill Resort ten miles east of Wheeler's Point, a lot easier due to the border crossing. The resort owner took quite an interest in our adventure and had us delay our departure long enough for him to get his camera. While we packed, he told us of a couple guys who left there on their way to Hudson Bay a few years back, "Didn't make it past Norway House."

We thanked the man for the use of his dock, thanked Joan for the ride, and away we went, north and to the east across Lake of the Woods from one island to the next, avoiding the nuisance of the northwest wind as much as possible. The next target for us was Kenora, Ontario, seventy plus/minus miles away.

Lake of the Woods (French: *Lac des Bois*) sprawls across parts of Ontario and Manitoba in Canada and Minnesota on State side. It is fed by the Rainy River, Shoal Lake, Kakagi Lake and other smaller rivers. Lake of the Woods is over seventy miles long and wide, and contains more than 14,552 islands and 65,000 miles of shoreline. It would amount to the longest coastline of any Canadian lake, except that the lake is not entirely within Canada. The lake drains into the Winnipeg River and then into Lake Winnipeg. Ultimately, its outflow goes north through the Nelson River to Hudson Bay.

"A river does not just happen;
it has a beginning and an end.
Its story is written in rich earth, in ice,
and in water-carved stone,
and its story as the lifeblood of the land
is filled with color, music and thunder."
Andy Russell, The Life of a River

Weeks earlier, in the planning stages, I had taken time to lay out our entire route across the lake with a number of GPS waypoints spaced a few miles apart. I marked up two copies of the necessary sections printed from the electronic version of the topo maps, one for Ed and one for myself. Using my GPS and Ed's map reading skills, we navigated our way at an amazingly steady pace around one island after another, across small bays, large bays, and countless peninsulas. Perhaps we were too confident and needed a lesson in humility. Late in the afternoon we found that we had paddled deep into a bay when we thought we had been paddling between two islands. As they say, "It can happen to the best of them." Ed just proved it. A quick portage (or should I say, a bushwhacking) through the trees was reasoned to be faster for us than having to backtrack.

Throughout the day, low marshy shoreline transformed into high banks and hardwoods. Now as evening drew near, the hardwoods gave way to granite lacing along the water's edge, almost all of it undeveloped. We were being awed by much of the same scenery the early explorers of this region saw when they first set eyes on this island-studded treasure located in the middle of the continent.

This was our first day back on the water, and big water it was, so we did not want to risk trying to locate a campsite after dark. An hour before it was too late, Ed and I began scrutinizing the options; too much high grass, not enough fuel supply, or too close to heavy spruce – mosquito habitat. As long shadows were being created, we spotted a very small island, perhaps a hundred yards in diameter, with a vacant cabin and enough mowed grass for a couple of tents. It looked extremely enticing. Directly across from the cabin was a small east-facing sand cove, bordered on the backside with a granite hedge. Huge red pine reaching up a hundred feet or more stood proud along the crest of hillside against a steep elevation. As we beached in the cove in the shadows of the giant conifers, two power boats raced by, interrupting our slice of tranquility, hopefully heading off the water for the evening. Two loons bid them a farewell. One could almost sense a bit of cynicism in their call.

Ed and I set up our tents, made dinner, and filtered water for the start of the next day before settling down. Ed brought two water filters for the trip, one with a sand filter and the other using a charcoal filter. This is one trip where we don't have to carry our own fresh water or need to rely on wells at DNR campsites. The filters will protect us from microscopic flagellated protozoan parasites that could be in the water that could result in giardia. Symptoms of giardia include bloating, fatigue, and sometimes vomiting combined with diarrhea. None of which are welcome when in the comfort of your own home much less while on a multi-week excursion where the closest urgent health care center could be a couple hundred miles "*over there*" through wilderness.

Graced by a greeting of clear skies, we were up before 5:00 a.m. and on the water in forty-five minutes. Off to a great start; meandering around dozens of small islands. If it were not for the topo maps and the GPS, we (or at least, I) would have lost the way within minutes. But what an incredibly beautiful backdrop to become lost in – a temperature in the low forties, blue sky, a heavy mist hanging over the flat water, while a half dozen loons welcome the day, doing their best to harmonize with local ducks and geese in somewhat of an un-orchestrated antiphon. Life on the water – life abundant.

After two miles of paddling we encountered a portage with a boat ladder. It was the first of many we came across that made portaging a bit easier. This one actually had iron rails, a dolly on wheels, and a winch to aid in moving larger crafts. The railway portage allows larger boats to be positioned onto the dolly then winched up and over the embankment. Other boat ladders we found were made of wood, long timbers or logs running perpendicular to the shoreline with shorter cross-members secured to the two "rails" making a boat ladder on which the watercraft could be dragged up more easily than over the terrain. Rope and pulleys sometimes replaced the use of a winch to help with larger crafts. In the absence of any mechanical assistance, brute strength was the only source of power.

On the opposite side of this particular portage we entered the crystal clear waters of the Indian reservation on Whitefish Bay. A large sign, perhaps four feet by six feet, assured us that we had made the right choice in camping where we did the night before. "No Trespassing! No Camping! A substantial fine is possible for camping within a half-mile of the water's edge."

In the late afternoon a southeast wind gave reason to put the sail up on my kayak, giving the paddle a rest for a good three miles or so. Conditions allowing the use of a sail do not come very frequently; when they do, you have to take advantage. Generally, I have found that a sail on a kayak is more of a nuisance than anything. For whatever reason, I continue to bring one on excursions hoping to prove myself wrong. I doubt it will ever happen.

"Disappointment to a noble soul
is what cold water is to burning metal.
It strengthens, tempers, intensifies, but never destroys it."
Unknown

Too soon, the afternoon gave way to evening and we were once again in search of a campsite, forty-two miles from our last campsite. Shortly after eight o'clock we set camp on the north end of a rock-of-an-island that created a five-plus acre refuge a couple of miles off shore; us on one end and an empty cabin on the other. Abrupt ledges along the shore make for a difficult exit from a kayak, and a much more difficult re-entry. However, sometimes there is simply no other choice. As we balanced precariously between our kayaks and the rocks standing on legs stiff from sitting all day, we fully expected to create a scene worthy of a grand prize on Funniest Home Videos. Somehow, we were spared.

Our last night on Lake of the Woods was bug-free with a sky as clear as it was when we began this day nearly sixteen hours earlier. End-of-the-day chores had already become routine; erect tents, gather firewood needed for the evening with enough for morning too, filter water, make dinner, sponge out the kayaks, and call home. Cell phones would have been useless in this country, so instead we'd rented a satellite phone; not cheap but quite essential as far as we were concerned. I also carried a SPOT Personal Tracker to compliment the phone. This device allows the user to send a pre-programmed message along with a map and GPS location via satellite to friends and family to let them know that all is well. In case of a real emergency, the user can send an SOS to a response center located in Texas where the distress message is then passed on to local authorities in area in which the call originated.

Again we woke early, before 5:00 a.m. Unfortunately it took over an hour and a half to break camp and get underway. I was hoping we were not losing focus. Going into this, we knew we had only a month to make it to Churchill because Ed needed to be back to teach a class early in July. The schedule was tight. If we stayed on track, we would be able to spend a couple days relaxing and fishing when we got to the Little Churchill. If not, we would miss a great opportunity to tell and retell some of the greatest fish stories ever told.

Our course for the day was north by northwest into a 15-20mph headwind with a forecast including a sixty percent chance of rain for the following four days. A light mist hovered around us between frequent showers throughout the morning. Our objective was Kenora (originally named Rat Portage.) While planning, I did not have the same quality topo maps for Lake of the Woods as I did for the trek later on through Manitoba. The waypoints I had entered on the GPS for our crossing of Lake of the Woods was done by selecting a landmark on an inexpensive "fishing" map, then literally using a small ruler to measure distances to determine the longitude and latitude. From the time we launched onto Lake of the Woods to within a mile or so of the entrance of the channel leading to Kenora, the waypoints I had created had been surprisingly accurate. However, the last waypoint which marked Devil's Gap, and proved to be critical in locating the channel, was not even close. Ed was as confused as I was. The topo map was no help and the GPS was of even less value. Nearly an hour was spent zigging and zagging across the bay in a serious fog looking for the elusive channel. We finally spotted a guy working on his boathouse who held the key to unlocking the secret. Immediately we were back on the right path. Our crossing of Lake of the Woods was done in less than two days; a feel-good accomplishment even though I was beginning to have a bad feeling about our schedule.

The next thing to do was to stop at a marina. I had found it online in the Kenora yellow pages and marked it as a waypoint, confident someone there would be able to tell us how to get onto the Winnipeg River without having to portage through the city. At the marina we are told that Donny Big George was the guy we would have to talk with about an alternate route to avoid the downtown hydro dams. Donny, a local guide who's name fits perfectly, was a bit foggy on exactly where the best place was to crossover into the Winnipeg River, but he said he knew someone who had the answer. A few phone calls…

While waiting, Ed and I struck up a conversation with two guys who appeared to be more like permanent fixtures at the marina than haphazard customers. I didn't catch their names. Let's call them Pete and Re-Pete. They were dressed in matching well-worn Carhartt bibs, Cabela's rain jackets, and Maple Leaf baseball caps, all of which could have probably used an oil change. Perhaps they were independent fishing guides for the big lake waiting for clients, or more likely, just marina groupies. Obviously they were comfortable helping themselves to free coffee that tasted like it was concocted from the same formula used to create a sealant for asphalt driveways. Whatever their story, the pair had a powerful interest in our adventure and badgered us with questions about our route, gear, time line, experience, and anything else that crossed their minds. A copious amount of advice was spattered throughout the Q&A, including repeated warnings for us to be on the lookout for Sasquatch.

Another hour had passed with no paddling, but our patience paid off! Donny tracked down his friend and came back with the details.

"Paddle west five miles toward Keewatin. You may find it easier to stay on the left side for the first four miles or so. Then when you get closer to the Keewatin water tower, cross over and enter the channel on this side of the tower. The channel turns left soon after you enter it. Then take the first right down a side channel just beyond the marina which will be on your left. Go under the bridge. On your right, you'll spot a boat ladder that will take you over the levee to the Winnipeg River."

"Got it." We thanked Donny for all his trouble and bid him and his pals farewell. Across the parking lot at the convenience store, we purchased chocolate milk and a few snacks before we got back to any paddling, once again, in a light rain.

The cross over was exactly where it was supposed to be and exactly as described. This was a big load off my mind because as we were going into this whole operation, I had no idea how we were going to connect Lake of the Woods with the Winnipeg River. I knew it could be done, I just didn't know how we were going to do it. We went. We conquered. We felt good!

"It always seems impossible until it's done."
Nelson Mandela

It was a quick portage, dragging our kayaks on the rungs of the boat ladder up and over the levee. We were on the Winnipeg ready to begin the next leg. Half an hour downstream, two whitetail bucks stood near shore watching with curiosity as the kayaks passed. Looking at the topo map, the river resembled a cornfield maze. I was hoping the waypoint marked for our turn to the west was not off location. Ed reached the turnoff minutes ahead of me, out of communication range but still in sight. He did not disappoint me, with keen skills he made the exit from one channel to the other as if he knew exactly where he was going.

Mile after wet mile, we continued; logging in forty-two for the day before we threw in the towel. In between showers we found an empty cabin on the north end of Cummings Island, an amoeba-shaped land mass over five miles long, located on Sand Lake. It is one of the many lakes connected like dots by the Winnipeg River. A dock made slippery from the day's rain gave us a relatively easy exit from the river. We set up camp under the shelter of some big pines in the back yard. Our chores this night did not include gathering firewood. Nor did we dine together and retell the day's highlights. Once the tents were up, we disappeared and hunkered down for the night. The rain continued to fall, even as we packed up in the morning.

In Manitoba, the Winnipeg River is broken up by six hydroelectric dams: the Pointe du Bois Generating Station at Pointe du Bois, Slave Falls just a few kilometers downstream, Seven Sisters Falls Generating Station at Seven Sisters, MacArthur Falls Generating Station, the Great Falls Generating Station, and the Pine Falls Generating Station at Powerview, Manitoba. In Ontario there are dams at Kenora and Whitedog Falls. There are also many lakes along the Winnipeg River where the river widens, including Nutimik, Eleanor, Dorothy, Margaret, Natalie, and Lac du Bonnet, all in Manitoba. Nutimik, Dorothy, and Margaret Lakes are all entirely within the Whiteshell Provincial Park. Lakes in the Ontario portion of the river include Gun, Roughrock and Sand.

We were in our cockpits ready to go at 6:15 a.m. Within a couple hours we reached the hydro dam at Whitedog Falls. Scouting for the portage began. Manitoba Hydro does not make it easy for paddlers, no signage and no obvious trail. On the paved road leading to the dam, we found a sign pointing down a gravel forest road indicating a water access on the downstream side. We ventured down the road for a quarter mile or so before deciding we had no choice but to bite the bullet and begin the portage regardless how far it might be. At the same time that we returned to the kayaks, Sam, an iron worker on a maintenance project going on at the dam drove up and offered to give us a lift. We hoisted the loaded kayaks atop the rack of his pickup truck and away we went, over the hills and through the woods. The landing was a strong half mile away. The rain gave a reprieve, at least for a few minutes, giving us a chance for a quick bite before getting back on the river. While we were eating, the siren on the dam sounded signaling the control gates were being opened. The kayaks we had set on the beach ten feet back from water's edge were now under threat of being floated away. We didn't waste any time getting back on the river so we could take advantage of the extra flow.

The rain came and went throughout the day, as did any flow that proved to be a benefit. The headwind did not vary and was more than a nuisance all day long as we paddled across numerous lakes where the waterway expanded to over a mile in width. Between the lakes, the river necks down to meander and twist below vast walls of granite topped with spruce stunted by decades of severe winters.

The Winnipeg River flows 146 miles from the Norman Dam in Kenora to its outlet at Lake Winnipeg. The river's watershed stretches over 41,100 square miles, mainly in Canada, though 11,000 square miles are in northern Minnesota. The river's name means "murky water" in Cree. Natives used this river route for thousands of years before it became a major fur trade route. Flowing between what is now southern Manitoba and Ontario, the river provided a natural means of transportation back and forth.

Many petroforms can be found at Bannock Point where the Winnipeg River meets the Whiteshell River in Whiteshell Provincial Park. Petroforms are man-made rock formations on the open ground. Petroforms can also include a rock cairn or inukshuk, an upright monolith slab, a medicine wheel, a fire pit, a desert kite, sculpted boulders, or simply rocks lined up or stacked for various reasons. The Bannock Point Petroforms were created long before the first Europeans' visit. On no small scale, these boulders were positioned on mossy bedrock by ancient peoples in shapes of turtles, birds, fish, humans, and snakes. These formations were a way to teach the important concepts of four directions and astronomical observations about the seasons, and as a memory tool for certain stories and beliefs. Petroforms were a means to pass along knowledge and information, as well as ceremonial practices.

"Look deep into nature,
and then you will understand everything better."
Albert Einstein

Ed spied a campsite on the edge of an island before it was even eight o'clock. We had only gone thirty-two miles and it was early. On the other hand, we were in between rain showers, we were cold, wet, tired, and hungry. In short, we were miserable and not about to let this one slip away. It was a great find! The site had an elevation that provided a magnificent view of the lake. It came equipped with a makeshift table and supply of firewood. Over an hour of daylight remained and we did not waste any of it. A good hot fire was built to dry our clothes, while Ed made us spaghetti for dinner. The laundry and other necessary chores were completed ahead of the next rain. A good night's sleep did not escape us.

It was the fifth day since entering Canada and our third day in the rain. The good news was that the wind had diminished, and once again shifted to our backside. The bad news was we got off to a lazy start – up at 4:45 not on river till 7:45 a.m. The hydro dam at Pointe du Bois was twenty nine miles from today's start. Again, no signage regarding a portage. Again, no obvious trail. Our scouting began on river-left, bushwhacking our way through wet swamp and willow. After nearly an hour, we aborted the effort and returned to our boats to paddle to the other side of the dam.

We were still a good hundred yards off the opposite shore when a pickup truck pulled up to a small parking area next to the dam. I waved frantically to get the driver's attention. At first, I wasn't sure if I had been seen or not, then the driver got out and waved back. Excellent!

The driver, Kevin, worked for a drilling outfit making upgrades to the dam. He waited patiently for us to arrive and was even more patient while I told him our story. When I asked if he could help us, "No problem, I'll be right back."

He retreated to who knows where, but when he returned, he was pulling a boat trailer. Kevin helped us load our boats and secure them to the trailer then asked if it was okay if we waited for two of his coworkers who were just getting off shift. The two arrived in minutes, with pizzas! An engineer on the project had treated the guys to lunch. "Eat up. We've had all we wanted." Outstanding! It was four o'clock and we were getting breakfast, lunch, and dinner all at the same time.

The re-entry to the Winnipeg River was over a mile away, down a narrow gravel road, beyond a small cluster of very modest homes, and through a trailer park. It was a landing I doubt we would have ever found on our own. In route, Kevin told us of two young paddlers he had assisted last year who were on their way to York Factory in a birch bark canoe they had made themselves. Similar to us, he just happened to be at the dam to support them when they had arrived. However, they didn't want to risk damage to the canoe which they had spent 500 hours to build. The kids carried their canoe themselves while Kevin hauled all their gear ("at least 800 pounds!").

By the time we got back on the water, over two hours had escaped us. Four miles downstream, it was time for another portage. This portage was comparatively easy although it took over an hour to negotiate the trail through tall grass, up one hill, across a set of railroad tracks, and down the other side and then exiting near a small eddy on the river. Four more miles and we finally found an island that, from a distance, appeared to be suitable for a campsite. As we got closer, the abrupt granite outcrops on the upstream side looked like a landing we would want to avoid. Doing a recon to the backside of the island, we discovered a beautiful sand beach on the far end only a quarter mile away – much better.

A single loon mourned out a cry at 4:00 a.m., waking both of us. The bird may have awakened us, but did nothing for our motivation. It was another two hours before our paddles hit the water. The set of rapids marked on the map two miles from camp turned out to be a nonevent; no excitement; no increased flow. However, just beyond this set of would-be rapids was a waterfall that we thought would be best to scout before going forward. Another nonevent, it was nothing more than a few rocks and a gradual four-foot drop over maybe thirty or forty feet. We made it without a problem. Beyond the waterfall was faster water, good flow and no rapids. The shore could not have been more beautiful. Variegated granite outcroppings decorated with large splotches of pastel lichen poking out from a thick Christmas-green spruce forest lining both sides of the river. Neither the gloomy gray sky nor the drizzle of rain were able to distract from the magnificence of the landscape that surrounded us. It was a splendor available to so many only in magazines or through the artist's brush.

The miles passed quickly. Soon we found ourselves nearing civilization; a large resort, vacation homes, a city park and across the way was a golf course. We had arrived in Pinawa, MB, a welcome sight for two very damp travelers who were chilled to the bone. The boats were dragged up onto the empty beach near the swing set at the city park, and off we went in search of a hot meal, something that had not been freeze dried in another life. We struck it rich! The golf course had a club house with a restaurant and more importantly they seemed to be receptive to hosting two wet and smelly travelers. Our brunch was a long leisurely affair, taking time to recharge our "batteries" and those in the satellite phone as well, all the while the rain poured out of the sky.

On our return to the boats we ducked under a small wooden canopy to study a map of the area. While we stood out of the rain, strategizing, an older gentleman who was walking his dog stepped up. He and his dog shared an umbrella as he drilled us with questions. "Where are you from?" Where are going?" "Why?" "How long is it going to take to get to Churchill?" – The usual. As we told of our adventure, the old man's eyes brightened, a smile appeared, and in a few moments, he was standing taller and appeared years younger. Finally he stepped up to the map; then his tales unraveled. He drew with his finger the routes he had canoed with his friends many years before. Our new friend had paddled the area for many years and was extremely familiar with the dams, and more importantly, knew how to get around them. He explained that it was more intentional than not, that Manitoba Hydro had not created portages. They don't necessarily want to invite more traffic around the vulnerable facilities, many of which are unmanned.

The river flows west from Pinawa for a few miles before making a sharp sweep to the north. The south wind pushed us along with foot-and-a-half waves rolling up from behind. Coming up on the Seven Sisters Hydro Dam, the wind was no ally. With a safe distance between us, Ed and I cautiously moved up closer to the riprap looking for a place to land as the dark water reverberated off the rocks. Our boats were slammed into the rocks while waves washed over the decks and into the cockpits. On shore, the riprap was wet and slippery. However, there always seems to be a good side, if you seek it – we were in between rain showers again.

It seemed that the old man at the park had painted a perfect picture of the approach; more than a mile-long pool behind the dam, hydro dam on the left, a service road coming in from the east protected by a twenty-foot-high levee draped with riprap. "You'll see a hand railing near the hydro, on the right side, extending down from the service road. Pull up on the rocks, fifteen to twenty meters east (to the right) of the hand rail. Go up and over the road where you should be able locate a narrow trail that follows along the river. It's not a short portage, close to two and a half kilometers (about a mile and a half)."

Once each of us had our kayaks resting safely on the upstream side of the levee, we loaded our gear into the portage packs and got everything to the service road. On the opposite side of the levee, we found the slope was so steep that we had to use a portaging strap on the stern of each kayak with one of us on top near the road lowering the boat down the incline, while the other guided the bow over sharp rocks.

Then the "leapfrogging" began. Leapfrogging a portage is when you load yourself down with whatever you can carry, head out and go as far as you can, and when you need a rest, drop the stuff and go back to where you left your last load to repeat the process. The distance is compounded, but generally, there are few options.

Feeling proud of ourselves for making quick work of it all, we were all set to get to paddling again when I realized I had forgotten the small bag I had stowed in my cockpit. It was still back at the hydro dam lying in the tall grass right where I had left it. Just as I was about to leave to go back for it, Ed volunteered. He said his legs needed some running. When he was in high school, Ed broke the state record for the mile. The 4:20 held for many years. Ed still does a lot of running to keep in shape. He left and was back in less than thirty minutes claiming his pace was hampered by the rubber muck-boots he was wearing.

The rain commenced to fall once again as we pushed off through the bulrushes back into river's flow. The rain didn't stop, even when we did around nine o'clock near Lac du Bonnet, seventy crow-fly miles northeast of Winnipeg, MB. According to the city's website, "Lac du Bonnet is one of the most desirable places to live, work or play in Manitoba. Endless rivers & lakes, lush forests full of nature and beautiful granite hills make this the last stop on the prairie."

Our camp was set up on an extremely moist clearing overlooking the river where a placard stated that an old school had once stood. Safe inside our tents for the night, we called home and ate a light meal before shouting out a "good night" to each other over the sound of pelting rain drops.

If you're going to spend time outside, you may find the weather does not always take your concerns into consideration. That is unless you have an "in" with the government, which everyone knows, actually does have control over the weather. Otherwise, you will have to accept whatever Mother Nature hands out. There is one option though.

When I first met Ed, he told me of the many camping trips he had made to the BWCA. The Boundary Waters Canoe Area Wilderness (BWCAW or BWCA), covers over a million acres of wilderness within the Superior National Forest in northeastern Minnesota. The BWCA is renowned as a destination for both canoeing and fishing on its many lakes. It is the most visited wilderness in the United States. Overnight camping is limited by permits secured weeks or even months in advance of the seven-day forecast.

Ed told me that his first trip to the Boundary Waters was absolutely miserable. He went with such high expectations of blue skies, clear flat water, fresh walleye fillets for every meal, and more memories than anyone deserved in a lifetime. However, after four days of rain he packed up the kids and headed home, doubtful he would ever return. Sometime later... the brainstorm. His flexible work schedule and the fact that he lived within an hour's drive of the BWCA meant that he had an advantage over most others. Rather than scheduling a canoe trip and be committed regardless of the elements, he could wait for ideal weather then find a remote and less popular access point with open permits. He has had perfect camping weather every trip since.

I have to admit it is on the clever side, but I am not so sure I could get quality rest, what with worrying about what I may be missing – the gale force winds coming out of nowhere in the black of night, winds persistently stretching and pulling on each guy line, puckering the flimsy nylon this way, then that, just short of hurling it over a sheer cliff of razor-sharp granite. Or perhaps the deafening sound quarter-size rain drops make during their assault, and the hail that precedes the rain which comes with such mass it could easily shatter the windshield of a Honda Civic... but somehow your tent endures. And let's not forget the thunderous crash of trees falling all around your site creating tremors nothing short of a 6.5 earthquake, all the while you are praying that your small water craft, which you failed to secure, has not ended up somewhere outside of Kansas with Dorothy and Toto. As great as it is to return home from camping and having to nurse a third-degree sunburn, it is inclement weather that make the better stories.

***"Sunshine is delicious, rain is refreshing,
wind braces us up, snow is exhilarating;
there is really no such thing as bad weather,
only different kinds of good weather."
John Ruskin, author***

Extra clothes are my least priority when I pack for an outdoor trip, actually any trip I guess. I don't fret about the fashion police coming by my tent in the morning to see if I measure up to the L.L. Bean or Eddy Bauer standard. I pack disposable underwear, (which happens to make a decent fire starter by the way, but not for cooking). The point of using disposable underwear is the pack-size. A pair of disposable briefs come packaged about the diameter of a German bratwurst, only half as long. An extra shirt and one extra pair of trousers are brought along for that occasional trip into civilization, should it occur. For cooler weather, two sets of long underwear. One set is for daytime use, the other for nighttime. So, you may wonder, what happens when the set of clothes I am wearing every day become "soiled?" I bring along an eco-friendly laundry detergent. After my clothes are washed, I put them back on to dry. During my excursion to Churchill, I did laundry once every two or three days, unless it was raining. At each day's end, in the privacy of my own tent, I'd take a bath using antibacterial rinse-free bath wipes followed up with a copious amount of baby powder for that clean-all-over feeling. If a chill was in the air, the extra set of long underwear function as pajamas.

Morning "on the trail" brings on another ritual. Regardless how cold it may be, the first thing on my duty list is to secure my sleeping bag and my nightclothes, keeping them clean and dry. Next is to protect my feet from fungus by coating in between my toes with a liberal amount of petroleum jelly and baby powder. Then it's on with the trousers and shirt even though they may happen to be wet from the day before, or even worse, a little stiff with a touch of frost. It is out of courtesy for my fellow campers that I don't bellow out in anguish.

Now, the alternative is what many do. Put on clean, dry, clothes each morning only to have them soon get soaked as well. If the rain persists more than a day, the result is a growing bag of wet clothes and a diminishing supply of dry clothes. Seldom have I seen people bring along more than three or four sets of extra clothes. Often the rain lasts one or two days longer than the supply of clean clothes. It turns out, Ed thought my behavior was nothing short of crazy.

As I lay in my sleeping bag this morning building up the required strength to don the wet clothes, I tried to recall if this was the fourth morning in a row putting on wet clothes or the fifth. It really didn't matter, the pelting of rain drops had ceased sometime in the darkness. Now the noise was under the tent's rain fly where dozens of mosquitoes were kamikazing themselves against the screen mesh above my head. Working as fast as we could, we managed to escape unscathed and unfed too. Breakfast would be a snack while in route.

Our first portage of the day was ten miles downstream, quick and easy. The second one, not so much! It was a combination of carry and drag over granite and through undergrowth. Midway through the morning the clouds began to clear. It was time for lunch and drying our gear, three hours tick by rapidly. Shortly after our break, we encountered another set of "falls." It was a little more than the one we ran a couple days before. We scouted it, challenged it, and triumphed. Below the falls we were met by half dozen whitewater kayakers playing with their eight-foot-long boats in the standing waves amongst the boulders. I cannot begin to describe their astonishment when they saw Ed and me come over the falls in kayaks twice the length as theirs.

We ran one more falls later in the afternoon; very doable and a good time. Then as the flow slowed into a pool that stretched out several miles above the dam near Powerview Pine Falls, the headwind whipped waves close to two feet. In much calmer waters we made our third portage of the day. It was the last one on the Winnipeg River was at the dam that controls the flow into Lake Winnipeg.

It's a physical phenomenon that: the bigger the dam, the bigger the draw. I have paddled on the upstream of some dams where there is no way you want to try crossing within a half mile of the gates. With that being said, it is better to get on the correct side of the river as early as possible. On our approach, two or three miles away, I flagged down a boat load of teenagers and asked them if they knew which side of the dam would be best for a portage. The consensus among them was river-left, but they couldn't be certain. A mile later, I approached a father and son who were fishing from shore. The dad wasn't sure either, but thought he had heard at one time there was a portage on the left. We went river-left.

Barrel-size boulders littered the shoreline on our approach to an eight-foot-high wire fence forcing trespassing of any degree down a footpath well away from the dam. This is where we met Rudy, a young man from Hutchinson, Minnesota. He had left home a month earlier and was planning another two months on the trail, paddling a twelve-foot kayak. Right away I had a great deal of admiration for the guy. His original intent was to follow the Sevareid route to York Factory on the Hudson Bay. He started in Minneapolis and made his way up the through the Red River Valley, but when he hit Lake Winnipeg he discovered that his little boat was no match for what the big lake had to offer.

His new plan was to head east following the Winnipeg River upstream to the Rainy River and again paddle upstream following the voyageur water trail all the way to the historic eight and a half mile long Grand Portage. The Grand Portage, used for hundreds of years by Native Americans, European explorers, and the fur trading voyageurs winds through heavily wooded terrain rising 630 feet between Lake Superior and the Pigeon River on the U.S. – Canada border. Once on Lake Superior, Rudy was heading west down the shore to Duluth, hoping to arrive no more than twenty-four hours before he had to leave for graduate school. (I have hiked this trail with nothing more than a day-pack. I would not want to do it carrying anything more!)

Ed and Rudy exchanging addresses before we made our portage.

Before I went off to do any scouting, I asked Rudy about the portage that lay ahead of us. "It's a killer, the roughest one I encountered so far!"

I left on reconnaissance and when I returned, I told Rudy, "You haven't seen anything yet." Then I asked if he would like to join us and he actually thought about it for several minutes before declining. I think he was enjoying the solitude of his own adventure too much to give it up.

Our encounter with Rudy had been on the heels of the same weather system that had tormented the entire area with four days of rain and overnight temperatures in the upper thirties and low forties. I asked Rudy how he had faired. He said that he held up well. It turned out his philosophy was the same as mine regarding packing light and not wasting a set of dry clothes on a rainy day. He went on to say, "It takes a man of special courage to put on wet clothes on a cold morning."

Ah Ha! Score one for the crazy guy!

"My psychiatrist told me I was crazy
and I said I want a second opinion.
He said okay, you're ugly too."
Rodney Dangerfield

Ed and I completed the portage around the last dam on the Winnipeg River. It ranked among the easiest we had come across. It was relatively short, across dry level ground; a stark contrast from what we had been used to. At the landing on the downstream side we "helped" a couple kids catch a fish before continuing on towards Lake Winnipeg, yet twenty miles away. We followed a course tight along the east shore, trying to stay out of a serious headwind as much as possible. As we passed Fort Alexander Indian Reserve 3, our kayaks finally touched the waters of the giant lake we had read so much about.

It was getting late and we were tiring of the wind, so we began our search for a campsite an hour before the sunset. It wasn't until an hour after nightfall that we found something acceptable, a spot that wasn't strewn with household garbage or ankle-deep with sticky mud. Settled in for the night, the last task of the evening was to put in my earplugs to block out the sound of the crashing waves on the sand beach. The wind seemed relentless.

Lake Winnipeg, at 280 miles long and 60 miles wide, is the third largest lake in Canada. The lake's watershed measures about 380,000 square miles, and covers much of Alberta, Saskatchewan, Manitoba, northwestern Ontario, northern Minnesota, and North Dakota. This big lake consists of two basins, a large one to the north, and the smaller of the two on the south end, which is about a forth the size as its counterpart. The two water basins are separated by a land mass on each side necking the flow to what is referred to as "The Narrows." The Narrows are approximately ten miles long and vary from one and half miles wide to two and a half miles wide, with some vast irregularities of course. Because of prevailing winds from the north and the lake's long, narrow shape stretching out in a north by northwesterly direction, a strange phenomenon can often occur. In the right circumstances, the water level in the southern basin can temporarily rise up to three feet. This can take place when the north winds blow across the long open span causing surface waters to literally pile up on the leeward south shores.

An excerpt from an email received from one of the outfitters I had contacted while planning our trip, "*Just to let you know the current through the narrows* (between the upper and lower basin) *can be very strong if a North Wind was blowing. It pushes all the water from the North basin into the South and when the wind subsides the water drains back into the North Basin.*"

Other words of caution…I read where canoeists traveling the Bloodvein River to Lake Winnipeg can often wait for days to catch a ferry across. (In some guide books, it is not recommended to paddle across the narrows.) The ferries, though 90 feet in length, do not run when winds exceed 15 knots (17mph) because the waves can whip up to fifteen feet in just seconds.

Another day and another early start hoping to get a few miles in before the wind ramps up. On the water at 6:00 a.m. – too late. Our first GPS waypoint was twelve miles from camp, on the east shore across from the village of Traverse Bay. We didn't make it without a break. If anything, the wind that blew down on us this morning felt stronger than yesterday. After seven miles of swells over two feet, breaking into our laps across the spray skirt on every stroke, it was time for a beverage and a snack. We didn't bother pulling into shore but just bobbed around for awhile.

Our access into Lake Winnipeg had been through Traverse Bay, a thumb-shaped anomaly about six miles wide and just as deep along the southeast shoreline of the lower basin, twenty miles from the dam where we had met Rudy. Entering the bay put us 230 miles south of Norway House, where we would venture north on the Nelson River. Right now, we were not quite three miles into Lake Winnipeg and already needed a break! Though the forecast promised clear skies, the sky above was dismal gray as heavier clouds across all horizons appeared to be gathering together for more storming. Our break was quick. If we wouldn't have started paddling again we would have been blown all the way back to the dam.

Around noon, a trace of sun began to burn away at the gloom. The overcast may have been dissolving into a little blue, but the wind was still going strong – too strong for us to continue. We stopped again, on a long south-facing sand beach. While Ed cooked pancakes for us, I paddled out a hundred feet from shore to get away from heavy silt in the shallows so I could filter water. As long we weren't going anywhere soon, I strung a clothes line to dry our laundry. Later, we took a much deserved nap. By three o'clock there was a hint the wind may give a reprieve. But it wasn't until seven o'clock in the evening that we ventured out around the point where we found only a light chop across the surface.

We kept paddling until half an hour past midnight, almost three hours after the sun disappeared. With twenty-two miles logged in for the day, we turned out the lights at 1:30 a.m. on a soft sand beach shared with a dozen or more gulls screaming into the darkness for no apparent reason, "Mine! Mine! Mine!" Once again, I was glad I brought along ear plugs.

"It is not the strongest of the species that survives,
not the most intelligent that survives.
It is the one that is the most adaptable to change."
Charles Darwin

The new day dawned into a cloudless sky and a temperature close to freezing. The gulls that worked the nightshift had gone, replaced now with new dayshift personnel – crows roosting in the tree line, complaining more intensely about the cold temperatures than we were. A light wind blew down the lake at us for the first two hours before abruptly ramping up to 15mph according to the anemometer I carried on my deck bag. The velocity varied little throughout the remainder of the day.

At this point we had approximately seventy-five miles before leaving the lower basin and crossing the confluence of the Bloodvein. The seventy-five miles was split over two days. Paddling in tolerable winds, we maintained a distance of less than two miles off the east shoreline, while keeping a watchful eye on the weather.

Mid-afternoon of the second day, approximately fifteen miles south of the Bloodvein confluence, we watched with unease as a wicked-looking storm front moved from west to east over the narrows between the two basins. Other than the front dropping a little rain where we were and stirring up the wind, we didn't let it hinder our progress. Although, I have to admit I was giving a great deal of thought to what we had read in regard to the eight-mile crossing of the outlet of the Bloodvein, knowing we were coming upon it soon. The front continued to move slowly, perpendicular to our course, leaving behind a glorious double rainbow.

We actually found a favorable current in the narrows as we hugged tight to the east shore. The land mass on the east side of the narrows resembles a large arrowhead pointing straight to the west. That's where we decided to stop and make sure we were ready for whatever we found on the other side of the point. No sooner did we quit paddling than a fishing boat appeared, coming from where we were going. I hailed it over and asked about conditions. "Very little wind. You shouldn't have any problems."

That was not just good news, it was great news! Our timing could not have been better. We moved on around the point and began crossing the wide open span of the mouth of the Bloodvein on amazingly calm waters. So were our spirits. The eight mile paddle took a little more than two hours; a light rain fell till we got to the midpoint. Then within a matter of a few minutes, any hint of a breeze faded away and the rain clouds above seemed to simply dissolve into the blue. From the horizon to the north all way around to the southwest, it was perfectly clear except for a few remains of wispy clouds left behind to enhance the setting sun. Mother Nature's canvas was about to be painted with some of the most spectacular and vibrant colors available to her. It was breathtaking. An incredible sunset to the west, and off to our right, in the east, a full rainbow in all its glory. Ahead, on the bluff overlooking the Bloodvein, was an Ojibwe village. Lights from the streets and homes poked small holes into the beginning of darkness. We continued beyond the village searching for a quiet and secure place to spend the night. A small bay with a sand beach would do just fine.

Our request was soon answered. At the bottom of a shallow bay lined with a few spruce, we pushed up onto a narrow ribbon of sand beach. A beaver slapped his tail among the bulrushes, displaying his annoyance with us being where we shouldn't, mosquitoes swarmed out of the spruce to greet us, and a few dozen frogs joined in for no other reason than the fact that they could. Above, a waxing crescent moon produced a smiley face over the mirrored bay. It was all good.

For whatever reason, I decided to hike up the maybe-forty-foot sand embankment on the backside of the bay. I really don't recall why, perhaps in search of greener pastures. And that's exactly what I found, a wide open flat spot, mowed tight to the ground. I couldn't tell in the dark how far this field stretched out to the east, but it looked like a fair distance, at least a half mile or more. It took very little to convince Ed that we should pack our gear to the higher elevation, and out of the sand. Nearing midnight, we completed our nightly to-do list, including having a late dinner before crawling into our tents to give thanks for safe travel through another great day. The endless song of a whippoorwill lulled us into a deep sleep.

"GOD, my shepherd!
I don't need a thing.
You have bedded me down in lush meadows,
you find me quiet pools to drink from.
True to your word,
you let me catch my breath
and send me in the right direction."
Psalm 23: 1-3 (The Message)

In my years of camping, I have found that most generally there's a surprise of some sort waiting in the morning, especially if you've set up camp after dark in a strange area. Oh, what a surprise we had on this morning! There were our tents, as big as you please, anchored down on the end of an airstrip! Fortunately we were up at a little past four and on our way before getting in the way of any flights, coming or going.

Crossing the mouth of the Bloodvein River.

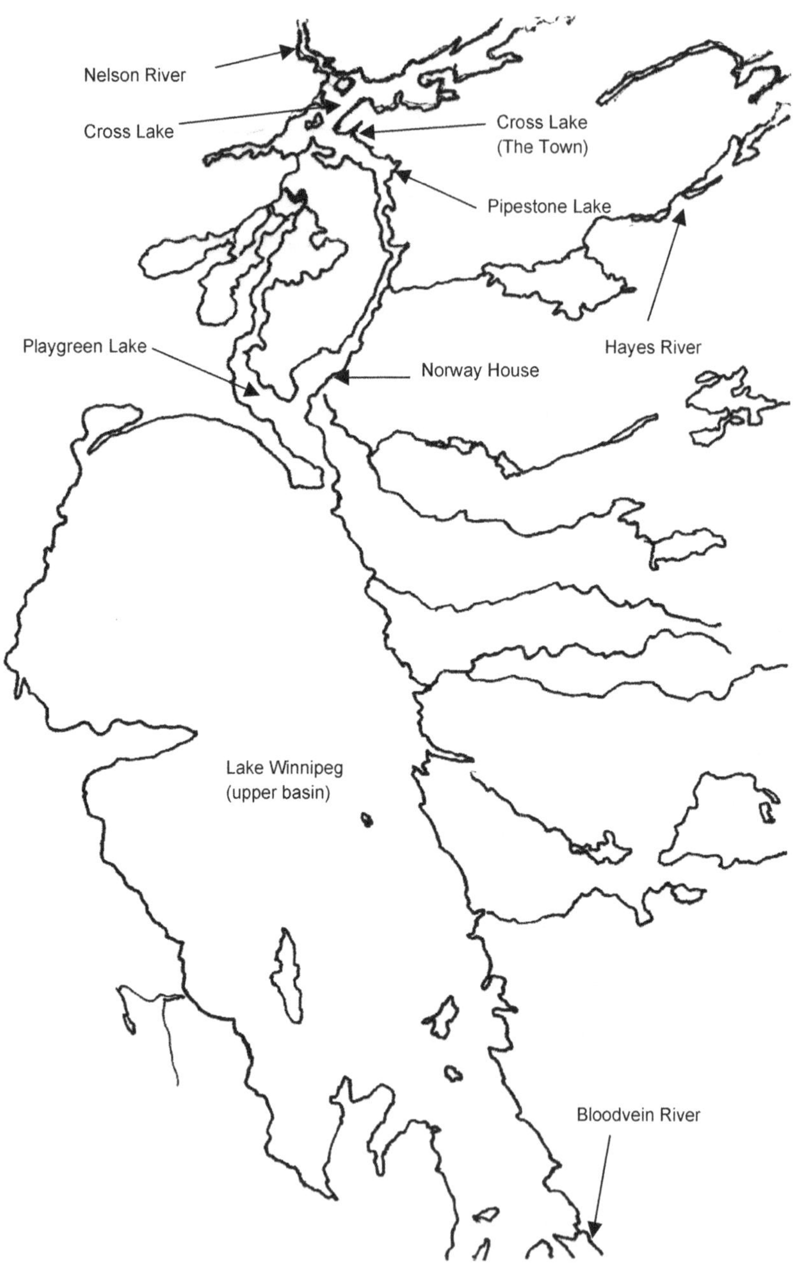
Nelson River
Cross Lake
Cross Lake
(The Town)
Pipestone Lake
Playgreen Lake
Hayes River
Norway House
Lake Winnipeg
(upper basin)
Bloodvein River

Bloodvein River to Cross Lake

Over the next two days, another eighty-three miles of Lake Winnipeg were left in the wakes of our kayaks. We crossed bays five to ten miles wide in up to two-foot rollers. Storm fronts came and went, churning up more rough water than we felt deserved, but we kept going. Periods of rain lasted anywhere from ten minutes to a few hours; winds ranging 20-25mph were more of a constant companion than not. If we thought the wind was too much of a risk to cross a bay at its widest, we would cut inland and make our crossing where it was a couple of miles narrower. People were nowhere to be seen. In the mornings, we would find fresh tracks near where we camped; moose and wolf. During the day, we occasionally saw deer, bear, and otter along the shore.

With each passing day, the wind got worse. On the third day, after we had camped on the airstrip, the water was so rough across the inlets of some of the bays that we were forced to follow the shoreline all the way around. Twice we paddled twenty miles into and around a bay to gain the five miles across. On the map, one particular bay appeared as a facsimile of a long accusatory finger pointing to something inland on the east shore. It was just two miles wide but a good five miles deep. We paddled ten miles to gain the two. When we got around to the far point of that bay and back into the lake, angry whitecaps whipped up by the northwest wind were waiting in ambush. Ed and I called a retreat. Ducking back in the bay, behind the point, we found protection from our assailant. The hard sand shoreline littered with driftwood and an old abandoned fishing shack out on the point made it the perfect spot to lay up for awhile. We had no way of knowing how long we would be staying. I had read of others crossing Lake Winnipeg who found themselves spending days killing time while waiting for winds to subside.

We secured our boats and went off to explore the fishing shack. It was a simple structure with its four corners resting up off the ground on two tiers of cinder blocks. There may have been a level involved at one time, but there was no longer any evidence. The one-room shack was around sixteen feet by twenty feet, with single wall construction using two-by-four's and wafer-board paneling. The floor was the same as the walls. The builders added a corrugated metal roof pitched at a steep slope from front to back, a window that wouldn't open at all, and a door that wouldn't close all the way; none of which did anything to add value. Not a pretty sight, and needless to say, Frank Lloyd Wright would have been proud not to have been connected to it in any fashion. Inside were a few things left behind from years before by who-knows-who; old magazines, a deck of cards, a ten-year-old calendar, and some, once functional, but now broken pieces of furniture including a couple of bunks with some pretty nasty blankets. Ed and I hung out inside for more than an hour discussing our options before relinquishing our homestead rights back to the shack's sole inhabitant, a mouse – a mouse, who had obviously never heard the possible results of curiosity. Back nearer the beach and out of the wind, we found two spots in the tall grass suitable for our tents. After so many short nights, we felt an afternoon nap was not out of line.

It was eight o'clock before the wind finally died down to less than 15mph. The decision did not come easy, but we chose to stay for the night. It was a relaxing evening, with a good sized bonfire and a quiet dinner of chicken from a foil pack, dressing and mashed potatoes. Clear skies won the battle over the clouds and allowed the twilight to last till 11:00 p.m.

I thought for sure I would find a heavy frost waiting outside when I woke at 4:00 a.m. I was wrong. An hour after wake-up, we were paddling with a stiff southwest breeze quartering us from behind and off to our left as we wove our way through dozens of small islands a mile off shore. On a few of the islands, massive granite boulders wrapped their way around small sand coves making ideal natural safe harbors. We hoped we wouldn't run out of them when it came time to quit for the day.

It warmed slightly through the morning as the skies grew dim with overcast. By noon we had gone twenty miles. After lunch, the wind continued to test our stamina, and toward evening, I recorded wind speeds of 25-30mph. The big lake was holding up to its reputation for being unpredictable. For us, we just paddled harder.

Our good fortune held and it was on one of those sand beaches where we pitched our tents. It had been a long seventeen hours since getting on the water this morning. The bad news was that forecast for the next day included more rain, so before going to bed, we built a fire to dry our clothes. Once again it was after midnight before we got into the sleeping bags. In spite of the wind and a few breaks, we had made fifty miles; only ten more to go before we could say we conquered Lake Winnipeg.

This was the sixth day of our 230 mile route along the east shore from where we had entered Lake Winnipeg on Traverse Bay to Playgreen Lake, our "turn off" toward Norway House. Accounts we read of other paddlers' experience on Lake Winnipeg told of being held up for several days due to excessive waves. We considered ourselves to be very blessed to have spent only two afternoons sitting out waiting for winds to die down.

The rain held off throughout the night and the morning winds were calm allowing us to make good time as we made our exit. On our way through Playgreen Lake, we encountered the first water travelers we had seen since Rudy, almost a week earlier. They were two college kids in a canoe, following the Sevareid route, of course. We tried to convince them to come with us, but they had been planning the trip for two years and were not about to deviate from their route.

Stretching out across the top of Lake Winnipeg toward the northwest at a forty-five degree angle, Playgreen Lake is about five miles wide and nearly twenty-five miles long. We made our cutoff onto the Nelson River some ten miles up the east shore of Playgreen.

It felt good to be on a river again, paddling downstream, and not having to worry about any rogue northwest winds coming at us across miles of open water. A short lunch break was in order, and a time to take in all of the splendor; the granite boulders strewn about, the smell of spruce, a deer on the opposite side of the river, and a beaver swimming across up ahead. Pristine was the only word to describe it.

We arrived at Norway House, MB a few minutes after five o'clock. We were hoping to do a little resupply, although still okay with most of our cache and could have easily gone another five days. Our plan was to resupply at Norway House all along, but then again we planned for having to spend a few "wind days" on Lake Winnipeg. The first grocery store we stopped at was closed. The second had all we needed including some treats such as ice cream and chocolate milk. There was no question whether or not we were deserving.

Norway House is a small rural community, with a population of less than 6,000, situated nineteen miles north of Lake Winnipeg on the east bank of the Nelson River. The community shares the name *Norway House* with the Norway House Cree Nation Indian Reserve. Thus Norway House has both a Chief and a Mayor. The plaque near the boat landing where we stopped read: *"Norway House – Built on Jack River in 1812-13, by the Hudson's Bay Company. It was rebuilt on this site in 1825 and was a frequent meeting place of the council of the Northern Department of Rupert's Land. Here the Rev. James Evans invented the Cree Syllabic System. In 1875, Treaty No. 5 was made here, whereby the Saulteaux and Swampy Cree ceded their rights over approximately 100,000 square miles in this vicinity."*

We ate our treats riverside and decided to hold off on dinner until we found a campsite. A light rain fell for only a few minutes as we got back on the river, but no wind blew. Three short miles downstream, we found the ideal spot for our campsite on river-left, a large granite slab perched in front of a dense stand of mature spruce. Tonight's fire on this clear and crisp evening was to keep the mosquitoes at bay. Dinner was at nine o'clock, lights out at eleven-thirty, and earplugs were deployed at eleven-forty. We were not sure if the beaver were splashing and slapping their tails because *strangers* were in their midst, or if they were just playing games with one another. Either way, if sleep was to come, earplugs were a necessity.

"I love sleep.
My life has the tendency to fall apart
when I'm awake, you know?"
Ernest Hemingway

After a very restless night, it was again the usual wake-up time. Our internal clocks would simply not give us a break, and now the sun was getting up even before us, stretching the daylight to as close to nineteen hours as you can get. It might be early, but life is good! This morning marked the third day in a row of getting up to dry clothes.

Today was a day for portages, four of them, not around hydro dams, but a means to circumvent the challenging flow of the great Nelson River! The first was to circumvent a set of rapids. The portage was not marked, but a trail nevertheless and easy to find. The second was around a small falls, made easy because of a boat ladder fashioned from spruce logs. Someone had saved us from dragging our boats over the granite facing up an angle of less than forty-five degrees, but about twenty feet high. The granite face continued up and over adjacent to the flow with another boat ladder downstream side. Here we were given quite a surprise. Walleye skins carpeted the entire face of the rock, at least thirty feet wide! Sad to say, we had already eaten an early lunch and it was a long time till dinner. More importantly, we simply had to keep going. There was no time to go fishing, maybe later.

The third portage was much like the first, almost in plain sight. However, the fourth set of rapids left us completely stumped. Ed and I scouted both sides of the river in search of even the smallest hint of a trail for a half an hour before accepting the only option; to "line" our kayaks downstream. Lining was something that neither of us had any experience with, nor were comfortable doing. Although we did come prepared and perhaps we deserved some extra points for that. We went ahead with a great deal of trepidation.

Several yards of nylon parachute cord was tied off at the bow and likewise at the stern of each boat. My kayak was first. Ed held onto the rope attached to the stern, steadying it in the torrent. I went on ahead with the lead rope; stringing it out around boulders and trees, then with shouts that could be heard over the turbulence, I called out how much line was to be released. While I balanced on the wet rocks, I guided the front end of my boat through the rapids, using the rope in one hand and my paddle outstretched in the other. It may sound a little insane I guess, on the other hand, what other option was there? The biggest concern at the time was losing one of our boats, and all that was stowed inside, in the process. It went well, though not so good that we would consider it anything but a last resort in the future.

Reentry after "lining" around a set of rapids.

Though we made four portages on this section of the Nelson, we ran several sets of rapids throughout the day to make life a little more interesting. Probably more exciting than any of the rapids was the sound of wolf pups barking and practicing their howl. We didn't actually see where the den was located, nor did we attempt to find it.

All the members of a wolf pack take care of the pups. Pups are born completely blind and deaf. However they do possess a keen sense of smell. The litter, usually four to six pups, is completely dependent on their mom and other wolves in the pack. The entire pack nurtures and raises the pups. When the pups are very young, other pack members bring food to the mother so she does not have to leave the den. Non-breeding females produce milk and males compete for their turn to baby sit. Around eight weeks, the pups are allowed to leave the den. Then along with their mom will join the others in the community nearby where they gather to sleep, play and simply hang out until the pups are old enough to go with the adults, usually six months. Around this time, they start hunting with the rest of the pack. Often, one of the adult wolves stays with the pups to watch over them. Enough said, if one of theirs is watching over them, we don't have to.

The last hour of daylight found us searching Pipestone Lake for a place out of the wind for our tents. In the final minutes of dim light, we settled on an island that provided a safe exit, but not much for level, smooth, or out of the wind. Pipestone, aka catlinite, aka pipestone, aka pipeclay is a type of argillite (metamorphosed mudstone), usually brownish-red in color, which occurs in a matrix of Sioux quartzite. This pink or mottled pink-and-white carvable rock was used by Native Americans for pipes and effigies. Tonight we'll use large pieces of rough-surfaced stone to hold our tents down as we roll them out, then on top of the guy lines after erected. Even with the rocks, it took the both of us to control the flapping nylon in the wind. Inside the tent I used my PFD to level out a place for the sleeping bag. Earplugs were once again deployed to muffle the strains of tent against the gale. No, it was not a good night.

"The pessimist complains about the wind;
the optimist expects it to change;
the realist adjusts the sails."
William Arthur Ward, college administrator

Entering the Nelson River.

Using a boat ladder at a portage.

A rest stop on the Nelson River.

Taking a break along a calm shore of Lake Winnipeg.

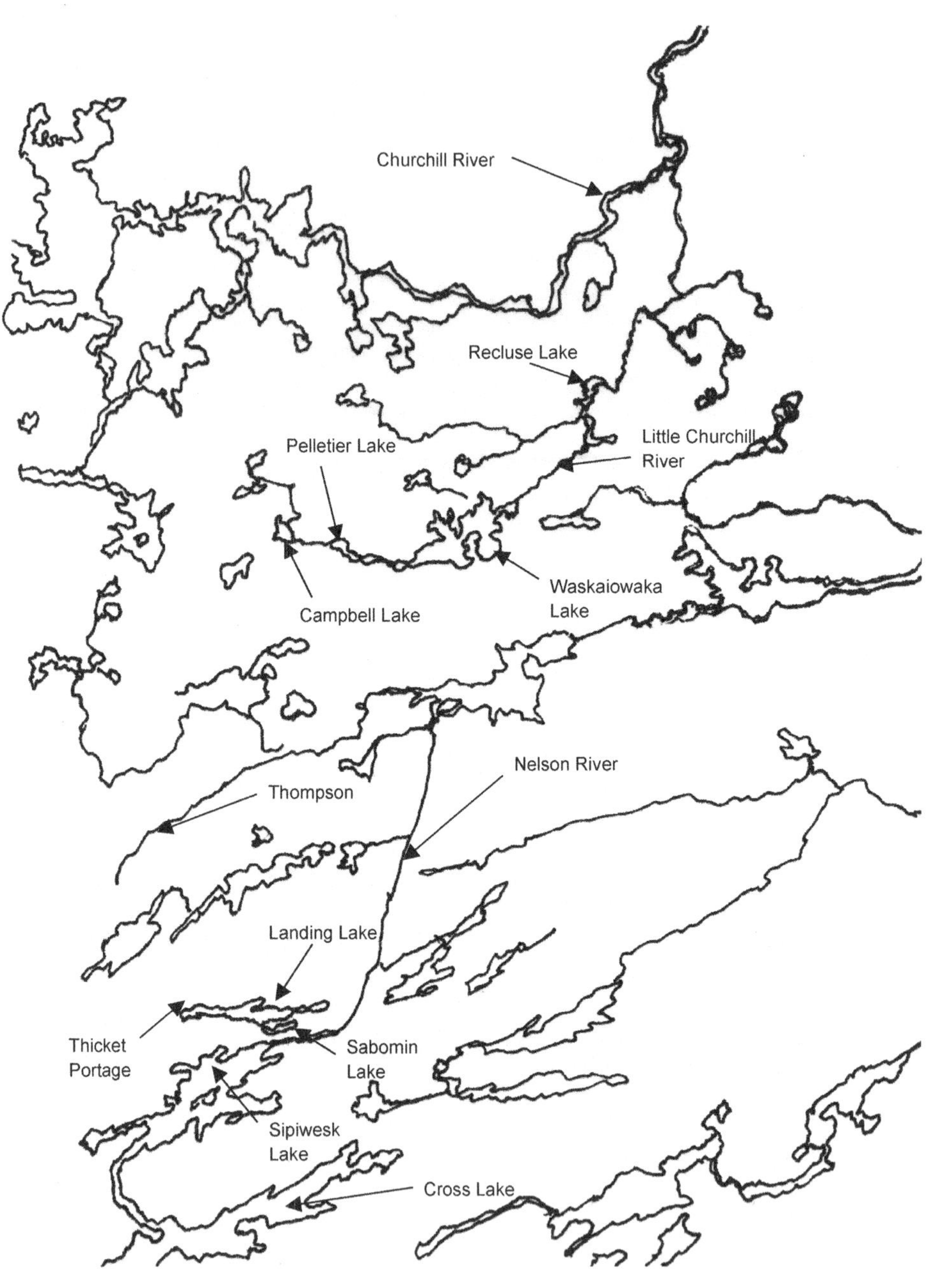
Churchill River
Recluse Lake
Little Churchill River
Pelletier Lake
Waskaiowaka Lake
Campbell Lake
Nelson River
Thompson
Landing Lake
Thicket Portage
Sabomin Lake
Sipiwesk Lake
Cross Lake

Cross Lake to the Churchill River

We reached the town of Cross Lake in the midmorning. On our approach, Ed remarked that he would like to stop if there was a grocery store. He needed a variety in his snack inventory, so we agreed that if we could see a grocery store from the river, we would stop. It was hard to miss, and likewise the park with a convenient boat landing. All our gear remained riverside while we went off to go shopping, less than two blocks away. As we were crossing the street, an old blue Chevy sedan with some First Nation locals squeaked to an abrupt stop directly in our path. Two rather round women were up front; three smaller versions of the same in the rear. The ecstatic driver had her window rolled down, "Are you the guys coming down the river!?"

In our conversation, we surmised that they must have spotted us from one of houses overlooking the river. They said they don't see many river travelers and were certainly surprised to hear we were on our way to Churchill; the passenger lady had grown up there. Over the next fifteen to twenty minutes, we told the rest of our story and listened to theirs before they wished us well and drove off. Our intent was a quick trip to the store. It wasn't shaping up that way.

We found things that fit nicely into our diet for lunch, so instead of going right back out on the river, Ed and I sat down at one of the picnic tables in the park where we had landed. We weren't alone but for a few minutes when another one of the locals showed up, a pie-faced man in his early forties, carrying a note pad and a pen. Carl introduced himself as a former sled-dog racer who now worked for the newspaper. He had heard from someone at the grocery store that there were a couple of strangers in town, "river travelers." Carl not only pumped us for information regarding our trip but he was more than willing to share what he knew about the area, and more importantly, the river.

In 1966, representatives from Manitoba Hydro, the Canadian federal government, and the Manitoba government agreed to proceed with the *Lake Winnipeg and Churchill River Diversion Project.* The scope of the project was to divert as much as eighty percent of the Churchill River's flow into the four-hundred-mile-long Nelson River for the purpose of providing flow to the hydro dams for power generation upon demand. Though the Churchill River (with its discharge of 35,700 cubic feet per second) had the capacity for hydro-electric development, it was determined due, to economic reasons, to further develop hydro dams on the Nelson River. The project "went live" ten years later in 1976.

The indigenous Cree and Métis people continue to feel the effects of this diversion. Water levels change constantly, eroding shoreline and destroying fish habitat. Carl told us that whenever the diversion is opened, Manitoba Hydro is required to notify the residents of the town of Cross Lake. The diversion is located on the natural outlet of Southern Indian Lake, over two hundred river miles away. They received such a notification two days before our arrival. The result… the water level of Cross Lake (the lake) which varies in width between three and four miles, but is over seventy miles in length, will rise two feet!

Effects of erosion along the shore of Cross Lake.

We left Carl and headed north by northwest, paddling a couple miles up a "dog leg" of Cross Lake into a light headwind toward the main body of water. There our route took a twenty degree course correction, to a heading of directly northwest. Four miles away, on the other side of the lake, we were to connect with a channel on the west side of an island that measured three miles by four miles. The topo map indicated a water fall in our path. No doubt, it will mean another portage. Ed and I paddled close to one another as we made the crossing toward our next waypoint. I was first to become aware of a low roar, such as a jet aircraft overhead. I searched the skies expecting to see a contrail left behind by a highflying jet. There was none, nor was there any other sign of aircraft in the blue sky above. We stopped paddling and listened. The subtle low roar was still present. And it was coming from the direction we were going. The two of us sat with our paddles lying across the cockpit cowling trying to determine the source of the noise when I discovered that we were moving. According to the GPS, we were moving less than 1mph into the wind toward our waypoint, the waterfall. The waterfall that was now two miles away!

It was time for another course correction. We turned and paddled northeast, toward the far end of the island, hoping to find an alternate portage. An hour and a half later, we began our search for anything that looked like a way forward. Two hours after our landing, we found what appeared to be a portage trail. Following it without dragging any of our gear along, we were led past the most incredible vista. There in a dense forest, the river cascaded over a drop of sixty to seventy feet into an incredibly beautiful massive granite gorge. The evening sun, low in the sky, cast warm copper tones over the tops of the spruce while a perpetual rainbow creating a prism of colors arched over an intense cloud of rising mist. All around us, the natural silence of night falling was under an assault from a thunderous roar created by tens of thousands of gallons of river crashing over boulders down through the chasm. It was a nice evening for a walk in the woods so we continued on. Nearly two miles later, we found a re-entry to the river on a sand beach in a quiet eddy. It was getting late by the time we returned to our boats, so we did the leap-frog thing for a mile or so down the portage trail in the dark before setting up camp.

This is as good a time as ever to mention that neither Ed nor I used an alarm clock on the trip, with the exception of one night, but we consistently woke within minutes of each other each morning. Our days were long, often not ending until close to, or after, midnight. But for whatever reason, as one of us would wake up in the morning, we would soon hear the other rustling around in his tent – usually between 4:00 and 5:00 a.m. One may think we were tough, late to bed and getting up so early; not really. It was cold every morning and when you get to a certain age, *Mr. Bladder* seems to be an excellent time keeper. Once you're awake, you may as well get up. Hard work and little sleep led to lower energy levels in the afternoon. Activity breeds energy! For us, we often chose "Nap" for an activity; worked every time. Besides, the afternoon temperatures were usually quite pleasant.

"Rest is not idleness, and to lie sometimes
on the grass under trees on a summer's day,
listening to the murmur of the water,
or watching the clouds float across the sky,
is by no means a waste of time."
John Lubbock, British Statesman

We completed our portage across the island the next morning under clear skies. Once again in the river with plenty of flow, the five miles to our next portage took less than an hour. This one was easy enough to find and we wasted no time exiting the kayaks on the sandy shore near the wide trailhead. Then our noses caught a hint of fresh blood. Slightly off the trail was an extremely fresh gut pile, likely from a young moose. A few flies were already gathering for breakfast as we scurried on past without stopping to investigate. The portage was relatively quick and easy. The hard part came at the end when we had to lower our kayaks down a ten-foot-high rock ledge to a narrow granite shelf resting inches above the water line.

Three hours into the day's paddle, we found the perfect spot to set up Ed's stove to cook eggs that he had purchased while at the grocery store in Cross Lake. There we were, two wilderness travelers taking a break along water's edge beneath blue sky with kayaks dragged up onto the gravel beach among a scattering of driftwood, a Coleman stove and frying pan being put to good use. It was a Field & Stream *cover-shot* if there ever was one. After an hour, the difficult decision was made to get back in the kayaks and go at it again.

We no sooner got underway, when a big aluminum fishing boat approached from the east and pulled along side. "Hello. Welcome to our country. My name is Leon. This is my friend Jeremy. What are your names?"

Ed and I introduced ourselves. Then of course, they wanted to know where we came from and where we were going. Somewhere towards the end of the conversation, Leon asked, "Did you come across the portage [waving off in the direction we had been earlier]?

"Yes."

"Did you see the moose at the start of the portage?"

"We saw what was left of a moose."

A slight hint of a smirk appeared on Leon's lips as he said, "Oh. There was a lit'tle moose there this morning when Jeremy and I came by."

Without confirmation, we knew what had happened and let it go at that. They wished us well and we bid them a good-bye.

Ed and I left our new friends and continued paddling around the many islands that dot the last few miles of the Nelson River before it widens into Sipiwesk Lake. We hit three sets of rapids. We ran the first without scouting. The second set we avoided by dragging our loaded boats across a small peninsula and then somehow managed to safely launch back into some pretty disorderly waters. In minutes, we found ourselves at the head of yet another set of rapids that definitely deserved scouting.

As I stated earlier, the MN DNR identifies river flow over rocks and boulders producing waves up to three feet as a Class II. A Class III is defined as "difficult rapids with high, irregular waves capable of swamping an open canoe. Narrow chutes may require extensive maneuvering. This is usually considered the limit for an experienced paddler in an open canoe." A Class IV is "long, turbulent rapids with high, irregular waves, including constricted passages and blind drops. Decked canoes and kayaks only; open canoes should be portaged."

Scouting a set of rapids.

Before starting this trip, I assured Ed I would not ask him to do anything he was not comfortable doing. So as we stood high on the boulders overlooking this set of rapids, we agreed it was a solid Class III, more likely a Class III-plus, falling just short of a Class IV. I turned to Ed and told him it was up to him. He looked hard at the craziness of the river, jumped over to another bolder for a better view, and then to another to study it more, while I awaited his decision.

Patiently… I waited as the minutes slipped by… then he turned back towards me with a big smile and said, "Let's do it!"

I went first, down the primary chute, looking out ahead for the haystacks rising ahead of the submerged boulders as tons of water-per-second thrash around me. It was one trough, then another, seeking out the dark water, making sure course corrections were done quickly and well ahead of the next obstacle; rudder to the right, rudder to the left, hard forward strokes, a quick back stroke to assist the rudder, then forward hard again. It seemed endless, but the ride was over in a few minutes. I found an eddy on river-left so I could reposition my bow upstream in order to get a couple photos of Ed on his way down. From his years of canoeing, he could read the rapids as good as anyone. He came quickly into view, then in midstream of the river his head went out of sight just as I had released the shutter. I lowered the camera to see what was going on and up he came again. I thought he maybe had rolled, but then realized he disappeared because the waves were above his head. Ed successfully finished the run smiling from ear to ear. I paddled out from the eddy to join him, knowing we were more than ready for anything out ahead.

"Some people are brave,
others are just too stupid to be afraid."
Philip R. Breeze, author

Sipiwesk Lake, Sabomin Lake, and Landing Lake lay atop one another on the map; all run east-west with a land mass of various widths separating them. Crossing between the lakes at the shortest points, and on established portage trails, meant we had to paddle thirty-two miles east on Sipiwesk, portage to Sabomin and continue east again four more miles. Then portage to Landing Lake, only to head west eighteen miles to the village of Thicket Portage, where our plan was to catch the train to Thompson, MB. The reason for the train was that I could not find a suitable waterway from Landing Lake to the where we could connect to the Little Churchill River eighty-seven miles to the north. Once in Thompson, we'd board a floatplane to fly to where we could once again begin paddling.

We entered Sipiwesk Lake late in the day, facing waves of one and two feet. After six miles of an uphill battle we found a campsite on a horseshoe-shaped sand beach along the east shore; less than an hour before midnight.

Nothing seemed to change from one day to the next. It was another short night; up at 4:00 a.m., once again putting on wet clothes as a result of having paddled in rough waters the day before. Need I mention how cold they were? The morning fire on the beach provided a bit of comfort, although we didn't stand around too long. We had about twenty-nine hours to locate and make the necessary portages and paddle the forty-eight miles to Thicket Portage to catch the train. If we missed it, we would have to wait two days before the next train would come through.

We were packed and paddling in not much more than an hour, targeting our first portage of the day twenty-six miles away. The water wasn't calm by any means, but it wasn't as bad as it was yesterday. Sometime midmorning, our spirits were lifted when we spotted a lone black bear near the shore. How can you not feel better when given the opportunity to see a creature like that?

Continuing to make steady progress throughout the day, we stopped only for lunch and one other short break. Twelve hours after we had wakened, we reached our waypoint, the portage on the far end of Sipiwesk Lake. The problem was we were there, but there wasn't anything obvious pointing us to a portage over to Sabomin Lake. The topo maps showed a faint dotted line between the two lakes, but that only means that there may have been a trail at one time, or it may even mean a "winter use" only trail. In planning, I identified that dotted line as a viable portage.

We beached on the soft muddy shore and began the quest. Ed went one direction, poking around the base of the high ground rising up from the swamp that ran along the shore of where the Nelson River discharges from the lake. I moved back up the lake fifty yards or so to see if there may be a trail directly over the high ground. After a half an hour of finding absolutely nothing, we gave up on locating the trail and decided instead to search for the easiest way to bushwhack our way through the swamp and forest. A breath away from making the final decision, Ed spotted something hanging about head-high from a lifeless old spruce twenty yards away, almost directly in front of where we had left the kayaks at the edge of the swamp. It had to mean something! We walked over to find a small white plastic lid from who-knows-what kind of container stuck over the end of a branch of the dead tree. Thirty feet farther into bog, along the very edge of the swamp, were two logs strategically placed crossways of a muddy patch. Pushing on through the brush after crossing the logs, we found the trail!

Neither of us had any doubt this trail would lead us to Sabomin Lake, so we opted not to fritter away more time exploring other options. The kayaks were completely unloaded in order to make the dragging process a little less difficult. Back home, in the planning stages, I had fashioned two fifteen-foot long nylon hold down straps to be used for just such an occasion. Each of the inch-wide straps was equipped with two snap hooks that could quickly be attached to the kayak's carrying handle. An eighteen-inch piece of nylon tubing slid over the strap made it ergonomically pleasing on the hand. The spring lock on the strap made the straps adjustable in length. (We could either hook two straps on one kayak to pull in tandem, or each of us could use a strap to drag. Earlier when we were making a portage over a steep embankment we had a strap connected to each end of a kayak as we negotiated the up and down.) These things worked great!

Ed and I each had two portage packs and one kayak. Let the leapfrogging begin! Let the feeding frenzy begin! The spruce-lined trail was soft, padded deep with sphagnum moss. Each step released an unbelievable number of starving mosquitoes armed with heat-seeking technology and extremely sensitive thermal receptors able to zero in with deadly accuracy. Haste was the name of the game. We carried our packs down the trail at least three-quarters of a mile, which we assumed was about the halfway point, before turning back for the next load, swinging and swatting. So far the trail wasn't under water, not to say the last half wouldn't be. The second set of portage packs made it on the next trip, the kayaks came on the third trip. Then the process began again for the second half. Overall the portage was one and a half miles; leapfrogging brought the number of miles to seven and a half. Our boots sunk in the spongy moss ankle to calf deep with each step, but never into water. That was the good news. The bad news was we had just spent an agonizing two and a half hours of up close and personal time with millions of *Aedes aegypti*, aka rotten little pests, in their relentless pursuit of the perfect blood-host.

We broke records repacking our gear and getting back in the water. No point in getting any more welts than necessary. Sabomin Lake treated us well. The four miles across the flat water took not much more than an hour. Problems arose when we again could not spot the portage I had marked on the GPS. My guess is that it had not been used for many years and was grown over. The water along the more than two-foot high bank was as deep as the bank was high, making it a little difficult to just jump out and start scouting the thick undergrowth. Even though it was only a half mile between Sabomin and Landing, we wanted to make sure there actually was a trail before making a risky exit from our kayaks. Finally I decided to simply trust the waypoint I had put in and go for it. Good decision. The grassy trail soon opened up beyond the water's edge and was wide enough for both Ed and me to walk side by side pulling one kayak at a time, fully loaded.

We dropped into Landing Lake on a small five-acre backwater created by the beaver dam, a work in progress that guarded the entrance to the greater lake. Approaching it hard and fast we were able to slide most of the way across. A good push on the end of the paddle and some enthusiastic scooting on our behalf completed the move. The call of loons coming from far down the lake seemed to be signaling the end of another day. It was nearing eleven o'clock and it wouldn't be long before the sun would be silhouetting the faint hint of the tree line to the northwest. We were on the east end of Landing Lake in northern Manitoba on the fifty-fifth parallel of latitude. The date was June 24, three days after the summer solstice, when the sun is furthest to the north creating the longest day of the year. To make our situation even more perfect, we were graced with a perfectly clear sky and a rising full moon.

"We need to find God,
and he cannot be found in noise and restlessness.
God is the friend of silence.
See how nature - trees, flowers, grass- grows in silence;
see the stars, the moon and the sun,
how they move in silence...
We need silence to be able to touch souls."
Mother Teresa

Thicket Portage was a leisurely eighteen miles away, all the way down on the west end of the lake. We paddled and we drifted, we snacked and we visited. All night long, the moon hovered over the trees to our left while the horizon in the distance to our right was illuminated by the midnight sun as the temperature continued to drop. When we reached the boat landing at Thicket Portage, we had been up for twenty-four hours. My hands were so cold and stiff I needed help from Ed to open a package of ramen soup for breakfast.

I can't explain the logic we used in making our next decision, but looking back, I'm not sure there was any logic. We knew the train station was in town somewhere. What we did not know was how far it was into town, or how large or small the town was. But we were about to find out. Even though we knew all our gear had to be transported into town, we left everything shore-side while we took off walking, carefree and empty handed. Maybe we were hoping to be offered a lift by an extremely hospitable local out driving around in an empty pickup truck. Of course the likelihood of that happening at 4:30 a.m. was probably the most impractical expectation one could have.

Thicket Portage was a mile and a half away from the boat landing, although there was a road from the lake into town, and a few unpaved city streets laid out in a grid as we got closer, we discovered later that there are no roads leading into or out of town. The railroad is all there is during the summer. In the winter, snowmobiles complement the train. Besides the railway station, which was the size of a single stall garage, there were a few small homes and a post office that looked more like a garden shed. Short of knocking on doors, we came to the conclusion that no one was going to get out of bed to give a hand with our gear so we turned around and sauntered on back to the boat landing. Let the leapfrogging begin! Another seven and a half miles of carry, drop, go back, pick up, carry, drop. This was on top of our mile and a half morning stroll into town, and on top of being up paddling all night. Ah, but it was a beautiful night and an experience I would not trade away for anything.

The 9:30 a.m. train arrived an hour late, not only giving us the opportunity to catch some zzz's on the loading platform in the morning sun, but time for the postmaster to rustle up some popsicles for us. It was his idea and certainly a mighty nice gesture on his part.

A crowd of nearly two dozen folks had gathered by the time the train arrived. The train's tardiness did not appear to surprise anyone, neither the locals nor us. Some of those gathered were planning to leave on a trip, others came to see them off or perhaps were there to meet someone who was arriving. One thing everyone had in common was they were all excited about Ed and me being there and where we were headed. When the train halted, two guys from the crowd ran up to open the door on the boxcar, and four others came forward to throw our gear inside.

The station never did actually "open." We got on the train without tickets and made ourselves comfortable, hoping to be able to settle up with the conductor before we fell asleep again. The conductor came by just in time. The cost was $21.00 each. That included our fare and our gear, a heck of a bargain for a three hour, thirty mile ride.

Thompson, MB, located 520 miles north of the U.S. / Canada border, is known as the "Hub of the North." As the regional trade and service center of northern Manitoba, the city serves a population of 13,123 residents and the surrounding area of additional 50,000 to 65,000 Manitobans. When we arrived, we weren't sure how long we would have to wait for our connection, so the first order of business was to find a secure place for our kayaks and the rest of the stuff that we didn't want to drag around while we were shopping. The conductor pointed us in the right direction – down past the parking lot at the depot behind a fence. The next stop was Baaco Pizza, then the WalMart. After our resupply, I phoned Chris at Venture Air, a charter service. He and I had been in touch a few times over the winter. "Just give me a call when you get to town, and we'll get you to where you want to go." That was weeks earlier, now Chris said there would be a delay. It wouldn't be until seven o'clock before he could get a plane back to the base. Due to the high fire danger in the area, his planes were up all day, every day, assisting Manitoba's DNR in locating any hint of smoke rising from below.

True to his word, two hours passed before a van with a trailer in tow showed up at the train station. Chris had told me he would have an Otter available for us. The de Havilland Canada DHC-3 Otter is a single-engine, high-wing, propeller-driven, short take-off and landing aircraft. Similar to its little brother, the Beaver, the Otter is ideal for moving people and cargo in and out of the hundreds of thousands of square miles of undeveloped Canadian wilderness. The Otter has a larger cargo capacity which meant that both of our kayaks would be transported on the same flight.

Our plane was just dropping out of the sky as we arrived at the sea base near the edge of town. We brought our boats and gear down to the end of the dock while Dennis, the pilot, refueled. The Otter has an oversized access door on the fuselage making it easy to load awkward cargo such as kayaks. Chris had mentioned in our planning that for our kayaks to fit inside the Otter, the maximum length should be sixteen feet. Ed's boat wasn't a problem. As for mine, I would just have to remove the rudder assembly; two bolts.

Dennis had a different idea. He would much rather have the kayaks lashed to the plane's floats using a bolt-on rack designed just for this purpose. It made no difference to us. We began to prepare our boats to fly, making sure the hatch covers, seats, and anything else that could disappear midflight was secure. Dennis used duct tape, inch-diameter rope, and nylon ratchet straps to hold them in place. It looked like the child's string game, *Cat's Cradle*, gone bad. With one foot on the dock, the other on the float of the plane, Dennis worked through it all, doing the double and triple checks, pulling on all the loops, snapping the straps, tucking in loose ends, and making any required final tweaks. We were glad to see he was taking such care, but I still had to ask, "Have you ever lost a kayak or canoe in flight?"

Without hesitation he cocked his head, looked up at me standing nearby on the dock, and with no emotion in his voice, responded, "This year?"

Our original plan was to fly north from Thompson to Campbell Lake, sixty miles. Ed and I had spent the spare time of this day going over our maps and our schedule. We had seven days before we had to be in Churchill to catch the train back to Winnipeg. No different than Thicket Portage, the train ran every two days. It was a given that if we weren't there in time, it would leave without us, and Ed would not make it back for the summer class he was committed to teaching.

From Campbell Lake, we were to paddle down a small river connecting to Pelletier Lake to the east. After crossing Pelletier we would then continue on another waterway to Waskaiowaka Lake and onto the head of the Little Churchill River on the far east end of Waskaiowaka. From Campbell to where we could begin on the Little Churchill was going to be nearly fifty miles of paddling. If all went well we could make it in a day and a half. The combined distance on the Little Churchill and the Churchill rivers to Hudson Bay was another two hundred sixty miles; a total of three hundred ten miles and only seven days to get it done.

We both knew that if conditions were good it wouldn't be a problem. If we had a glitch of any kind, success was not going to be part of the equation. The big unknown was the water level of the Churchill River, the last leg. When I had spoken with the conservation officer months before, he said that he has had many opportunities to fly over our route. "The Little Church shouldn't be a problem. You'll have a good time. That may not be the case with the big river. More often than not it's nothing more than a bolder field. I sure wouldn't want to be paddling it." Dang diversion channel! We had no idea how long it was going to take us and we didn't want to gamble. Our plans suddenly changed. Instead of Campbell Lake as our next put-in, we asked Dennis to fly us to Dunlop's Lodge on the east end of Waskaiowaka. Cutting off fifty miles of water would give us the edge we needed.

"There is nothing wrong with change,
if it is in the right direction"
Winston Churchill

Ed latched onto the jump seat in the back of the plane so he could take a little nap in route. Dennis said he wanted the pilot's seat and I took up the position of the Technical Air Crewman, the other seat up front. It was great to be able to get the bird's eye view of what we had been through. Countless splotches of blue water below nearly matched the acres of green spruce. While in flight, Dennis radioed Dunlop's to give them our ETA, nine o'clock.

I had had a volley of emails from Jerry at the lodge over the previous winter. His last message to me was, "Be sure to at least stop in for a cup of coffee when you pass through." The person Dennis was on the radio with at the lodge cautioned him of the extremely shallow water. The lake was at least three feet lower than normal for this time of year.

According to the website for Dunlop's lodge, *"We are the only lodge on this lake and there are no other outfitters for a hundred miles. The only way to get to the camp is to fly in on our private 3,000 foot airstrip [or by floatplane].*

The Little Churchill River system feeds some of the best pike fishing lakes out there. A fifty-five inch pike was caught at the outpost along with many forty-five to fifty-inch ones. On Lake Waskaiowaka, the number of trophy pike caught per guest is better than I have ever seen or heard of. All fish are released back into the water so that other fishermen may experience the thrill of catching trophy northern pike for years to come. Only small fish are kept for shore lunch."

We arrived at the fly-in lodge to be met by Jerry, his wife, his three children, four of his guests, and four others who played the roles of cooks and guides. They really made us feel special, everyone was standing on shore waving like there was no tomorrow. Dennis taxied the plane as close to the dock as he dared to in the shallow water. A guide named Thomas drifted a fishing boat out to the plane for us and our gear. Dennis slipped on a pair of waders so he could stand on the lake's bottom while he liberated our kayaks.

On shore, I asked Jerry if there was a place where Ed and I could pitch our tents for the night, out of the way. "Sure, but I don't want you to do that. We've got a cabin already set up and waiting for you. It's dry and has two bunks. Nothing fancy, it's one I haven't upgraded and don't rent it yet. We bought the place a couple years ago and have been busy getting things shipshape ever since. I'll have Thomas show you the cabin and where you can shower. Have you guys had supper?" The cabin was far more than we expected! Showers plus real beds equaled a real good night's sleep. We had also been told not to be late for breakfast.

"Hospitality, n. The virtue which induces us to feed and lodge certain persons who are not in need of food and lodging."
Ambrose Bierce, Author

By the time we went to breakfast in the main lodge, we had everything packed and ready to go. After Ed and I finished stuffing ourselves with pancakes and sausage, spread the handshakes all around, received a deluge of well wishes, we hit the trail. Our first stop was a hundred yards or so off shore to replenish our water supply. Jerry said there was no need to filter. His camp and all the guests drink right out of the lake. "It's never been a problem."

A half hour later, downstream in the Little Churchill, we found ourselves paddling right over hundreds of walleye just milling around above a small set of falls. Ironically during our planning discussions, I had been telling Ed that when we got to the Little Churchill, we were going to set up camp and I was going to perch myself on a rock overlooking the river and shoot walleye for dinner with my twelve gauge. Well, I don't see that happening now. Of all the fishing luck, eh? I had never seen anything like it, short of staring down into an overstocked koi pond. We had a big challenge ahead of us with too many unknowns to be taking time to do any catching. Jerry had asked about our plans. When we told him we wanted to be in Churchill in five days and absolutely had to be there in seven, he said, "Good luck with that! The fastest I ever heard that being done was eight days, most folks plan on ten days."

On the downstream side of the falls from where we spotted the walleye, seven otters, who obviously had more time for fishing than we did, played in the stream out in front of us. A mile further, we shot over a set of small falls without any issues except for Ed having forgotten to deploy his spray skirt. The situation called for a short break for him to dry things out. Fresh moose tracks were on the shore where we rested. Minutes after we were underway again, we spotted a moose standing near the river. The next twenty miles was a blend of rapids and fast water, no portages. After that the flow slowed. Then it was another twenty mile section with the river level low. We were constantly traversing about fifty yards from one side of the river bed to the other trying to stay in what little flow there was, often getting stuck in the mud or dragging on the gravel bottom.

Recluse Lake was more than simply a wide spot in the river. The lake spreads out across the map like a giant "S", measuring a little more than five miles from point to point. Along its scalloped shores are deep bays and jutting peninsulas, a topo map readers dream come true. Paddling into a strong headwind out of the northeast, we arrived at Recluse Lake in the early evening. During our flight from Thompson, Dennis had mentioned an abandoned lodge on this lake. This was the first season the lodge had been out of business. Likewise, a guide at Dunlop's had mentioned it too. We weren't sure what to expect so when we eyed a dilapidated shelter soon after we got on the lake we pulled up on shore to investigate. It was a pitiful site, garbage everywhere. Not an easy decision to go back out into the wind, but anything would be better than this. It may not have been an easy decision, but it ranked much higher than some of our other decisions. A half hour after the disappointment, we found the lodge Dennis had told us about. The uncompromising wind was whipping up whitecaps all across the lake in front of us. To make things even less comfortable, the temperature had been dropping since midday, now at least twenty degrees cooler.

Above the howl of the wind, we thought for sure we could hear the abandoned lodge shout out to us, "Come on in!" – in spite of the signs posted threatening would-be trespassers with prosecution. For those who could not read, primarily bears, unwelcome mats had been placed in front of the doors and below the windows of the five cabins and the main lodge. Unwelcome mats, AKA bear boards, are made of plywood with screws or nails sticking up every couple of inches spaced one to two inches apart. Properly constructed, they cause instant pain if a bear attempts to walk over the mat to reach a door or window, but do no permanent damage to the bear. An excellent deterrent, I suspect, even if the bear is wearing his/her work boots, the nails would most likely get the point across. Unfortunately Ed was not aware of the boards with sharp protruding nails as he stepped up to the door of the first cabin to read the notice posted by the bank. The good news was that the nail coming up through the bottom of his rubber boot missed his foot.

All the lodge assets were still in place and in good condition. The structures, the big aluminum fishing boats, even plates and silverware, it was all there waiting for the next person with a dream.

Asking for forgiveness, Ed and I made ourselves at home inside, out of the elements. I built a fire in the small wood stove while Ed cooked spaghetti for our supper. Outside, the wind was singing loudly through the towering pines, the sky grew darker than dark, and the clouds let loose in a deluge, holding nothing back. Inside, we rested with all we needed.

"The LORD protects the simple"
Psalm 116:6a

With the morning's routine completed, we paddled the remainder of Recluse Lake thankful the outraged wind of yesterday had calmed overnight. Now there was only a slight breeze to ruffle the lake's surface while the morning chill waited patiently to be tempered by the rising sun. Arriving at the outlet of the Little Churchill River, it surprised us to find it every bit as slow as it was the day before. We thought it would have been different due to last night's rain. But soon we had an elevation change and flow rate increased over Innes-Taylor Rapids. We shot it without any issues, a short fun ride and onto more fast water.

Another five miles downstream we encountered a larger set of rapids. This one required portaging over a long stretch of granite facing on river-left. We didn't bother unloading the boats. Instead we lifted on each end taking the weight off the hulls and skimmed them across the face of the rock. Before getting back into the swift current from the slippery footing, we took advantage of being on dry land to have a snack. At least we wouldn't be hungry and wet if we were about to be unsuccessful. We made it without incident.

It was turning out to be a strange day, weather wise. The calm wind of the morning ramped up by noon. The anemometer measured the wind nearly steady at 25mph with much higher gusts. The temperature was sitting at an uncomfortable forty-five under gray skies. The river kept changing back and forth between rapids and bottom-dragging shallow. Regardless, we weren't doing too badly. In the first five and a half hours of the day we had put eighteen miles in the rearview mirror.

We stopped again when we found shelter from the wind on a small granite outcropping under a backdrop of spruce. I prepared our lunch, mashed potatoes and peas. The remainder of the day was a repeat of what we had already done. The only thing different was Ed narrowly escaping an attack by two mute swans, similar to their cousins, the trumpeter, but actually more aggressive. He had paddled around a twist in the river, and without knowing it, must have ventured too closely the couple's nest. The female swam out from behind the bank of rocks near shore with a most belligerent attitude, actually almost running across the water, neck out, mouth open and hissing like she had a hair ball caught in her throat. Her gigantic wings flapping hard against the water were sending a very clear message, "Get out of here or I'll kill you!" It was about the time I came around the bend when the male with his neck stretched out to the limits began his assault with even more vehemence than his common law spouse. Closer to shore were the couple's two young cygnets making whatever preparations they thought necessary to join the melee.

From my vantage point it appeared that one of two things took place at this moment that saved Ed's bones from, sooner or later, ending up in the nest where they would surely be woven into the existing mesh of sticks and twigs. First, Ed may have simply gone beyond the imaginary security perimeter. Or it could have been that these two descendants of the pterodactyl caught a glimpse of me coming up from behind and simply lost their nerve when they realized the odds were no longer in their favor. Whatever it was, the command gave the signal to abort the mission and stand down.

Ed and I had come on this trip prepared to protect ourselves against wildlife attacks, but this particular scenario never once crossed our minds. However, it should have, considering swans can reach a length of over six feet and weigh upwards to thirty-three pounds. Their wingspans can be up to eight feet. There have been many reports of mute swans attacking people who enter their territory. Their wings are believed to be so strong that they can break a person's arm with one hit. On April 16, 2012 ABC News posted to their blog, "An angry swan is being blamed for knocking a man out of his kayak in a Chicago pond and then continuing to attack until the man drowned." I guess Ed and I were lucky!

We made forty-two miles by day's end and called it good enough.

Our bio-clocks must have gotten messed up somehow this morning. We didn't wake until 5:15 a.m., or maybe it was because it was so cold, we didn't let on to one another that we were lying in our tents awake, reluctant to face reality. Not only did we sleep "late", but we were extremely lethargic as well. It took almost four hours to get the kayaks in the water. Seems we didn't have time to fish, but we had time to make pancakes! Go figure.

The wind was once again calm. The riverbed was wide, perhaps a hundred yards or more. There were no steep banks, instead a gradual grade of rock and gravel disappearing into what was once a thick spruce forest, prior to a fire that took place ten years before. Now the growth of new spruce was struggling against the elements to come back. Spires of the dead trees, which were too stubborn to topple, stood over the little ones. In the undergrowth were hundreds, perhaps thousands, of wild roses. Their scent filled the pure air of our wilderness with a fragrance that blended perfectly with that of the young spruce.

Back at Dunlop's on Waskaiowaka, Jerry had mentioned that the entire area was experiencing a severe drought. Ice-out on the lakes was usually around the middle of June. This year, ice out was a month early. The weeks without rain after the early ice out and the June temperatures that were more typical of August were taking its toll. On the same day we arrived at the lodge, Jerry had received word from the DNR to exercise extreme caution at his outposts. The officer told him, "All back country permits are in the process of being canceled and new applications are being denied."

(I had talked with Jerry a month before, saying we would be arriving this week sometime.) Jerry informed the caller about Ed and me, "There are two guys from the States in kayaks on their way to Churchill. They are supposed to be coming through any day. What about them?"

After what Jerry said was a long pause, "Let them go on. But tell them not to have any open fires at all."

Our first thirty miles of this day was only slightly different than yesterday; chasing the stream's flow from one side of the riverbed to the other. Either it was bottom-rubbing shallow or Class I to Class II rapids.

Ed and I pulled up on the hard sand beach of an island for lunch around five o'clock. By now the temperature had stretched into the seventies, the wind had remained calm, and we had reached another milestone; the confluence with the (big) Churchill River. Not quite one hundred thirty river miles to the Hudson Bay at Churchill.

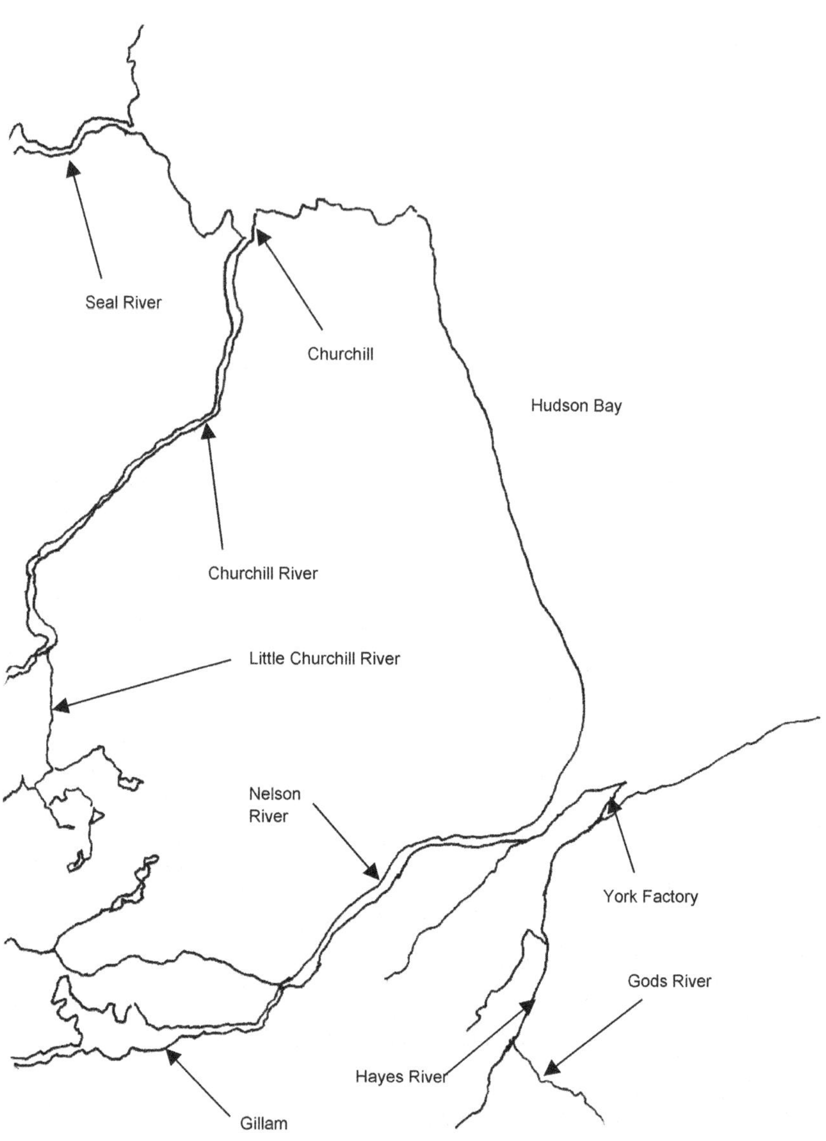
Seal River
Churchill
Hudson Bay
Churchill River
Little Churchill River
Nelson
River
York Factory
Gods River
Hayes River
Gillam

Churchill River to Churchill, MB

After getting on the Churchill River, it became deeper and wider, giving us good paddling for the next nine miles. Out ahead, around the next sharp bend, was Swallow Rapids. It looked like some serious elevation change from what we could see from the tree line, so we decided to save it for morning. It was ninety minutes until sundown but it felt good to get off the water early. As soon as we stepped on shore the mosquitoes became more of a nuisance than we would've liked, but soon their energy and the temperature dropped faster than the sun. We were in for the coldest night of the trip (so far).

"Happiness? It is an illusion to think
that more comfort means more happiness.
Happiness comes of the capacity to feel deeply,
to enjoy simply, to think freely, to risk life, to be needed."
Unknown

In the morning, Ed's gloves were found on the deck of his kayak right where he had left them, now stiff with a heavy layer of frost. Any discomfort was easily offset by the blue sky, song birds singing, and swift waters. Around the bend from where we camped, we shot Swallow Rapids without scouting. (Evidently a good night's sleep will boost one's confidence!) We felt like we could conquer the world. Over the next twenty miles the river twisted back and forth with good flow and two more sets of Class II rapids. Along the way we saw a cow moose and her calf. The cow, a bit shy, stepped off behind the undergrowth at river's edge. The calf was more inquisitive and hung around for a few minutes.

After twenty miles of more than adequate flow, the river suddenly went shallow. For the most part we chased the channel around piles of rock back and forth across the wide river bed. If it was too shallow to paddle, we got out and dragged the kayaks. Often times, pools to short to paddle were well over the tops of our fifteen-inch-high boots. We dragged over gravel, through shallow pools, and around boulders, hoping this was not a foreshadowing of what was ahead. One stretch of dragging lasted for more than a mile, right before we reached the confluence of the Little Beaver River. Then our kayak-pulling was over, at least for the short term. The terrain along the river changed abruptly too. The banks were no longer low, but now lined with limestone cliffs reaching straight up nearly a hundred feet, carved out by unrestrained wind and waters of years gone by. Spruce stood like sentinels along the edge high above us.

More flow meant more fun on the rapids. Once the Little Beaver joined the Churchill, we had a mile of good paddling on open river, a mile of Class I, a half mile of open river, a mile of Class I and Class II, then a half mile of open river. And more of the same for the next four miles; our skill sets and our confidence grew with each set of rapids. I was watching the GPS for elevation change while Ed kept an eye on the topo maps. We both knew what was around the next bend and that a decision had to be made. "What are we going to do at Portage Chute?" It was coming up fast!

During the planning stage, I had tried to find as much information as I could about various landmarks along the way. I found nothing about Portage Chute. Common sense would tell you that with a name like that, the best thing to do would be to at least stop and scout it. Well, common sense must have been stowed for the day because in an eddy twenty yards or so from the top of the chute, the discussion went like this...

"What do you think Jim, run it?"

"Let's go for it. We've handled everything else so far today. Do you want to scout it?

"I think we'll be okay."

"Alright, I'll go first. See you at the bottom."

It was settled, just that quick. In our defense, between the GPS and a quick view of the tree line, it didn't look like there could be much more than a thirty-foot drop. Certainly nothing very drastic like the chasm we had seen near Cross Lake. Otherwise, wouldn't this be called *Portage Chasm*? I gave a couple serious strokes to get back into midstream, sitting as tall as I could in the cockpit to get an eye on the deep black trough I needed. The trough was obvious and wide, almost as wide as the overall flow, perhaps twenty yards or more, but it necked down quickly between two sheer limestone walls. In the trough, the flow picked up velocity, and once in, there was no getting out. As the channel narrowed more and more with each passing moment, I gained a grasp for why it was called a chute. Perhaps we should have portaged!

The chute was flowing fast and there were no big obstacles poking out from below the surface as there had been in many of the previous rapids. It was simply turning out to be a fun ride. Then something I didn't expect! There in the very center of the flow, that now seemed to me wasn't much over thirty feet wide, and directly in front of me was a giant rock formation. Like a limestone Goliath coming up from the depths, lording over all who were foolish enough to venture forward – challenging me to make a choice, *right or left*. It was standing as tall as the flow was wide and big enough in diameter to split the river channel into thirds. The formation took up the entire center third.

For the first time in my life I realized how a squirrel must feel as it tries to cross the road with a car barreling down upon it. *Keep going? Turn back? No, it's better to keep going! Wrong, turn around!* I was in the same fix as the squirrel, trying hard to make the decision, right or left. The gap was closing faster than I could think! I thought to myself, "For crying out loud, the choice is simply binary. It's not like a real multiple choice!" As the milliseconds ticked off, my mind raced to come to a logical choice. Finally, like the squirrel, I decided. For no apparent reason I chose left even though I may have been a smidgen closer to the wall on my right. Regardless, the decision was made and

I proceeded to follow through.

The decision came too late. I was neither going to the left nor the right. I was headed straight, on a collision course with Goliath! Bam!! The front of my kayak struck the big rock absolutely dead center. It could not have been any closer. Normally the next thing that happens in a situation like this would be for the back of the boat to spin around crosswise in one direction or the other. In this case, my kayak was long enough, that in either direction, it would have blocked that half of the channel. Fortunately for me, my kayak was as indecisive as I was. The boat hit the rock with such a jolt, that instead of the stern swinging one way or the other, the entire boat was jarred backwards straight as an arrow several inches in the narrow eddy behind the rock.

It must have been enough of a jolt that it started my brain to begin thinking again, and I was able to take two quick corrective strokes and cleared the rock on the right. But it wasn't over yet. Once past Goliath, the elevation made an abrupt drop causing the river to churn and boil. I was hardly over my recovery of the collision with the giant when I entered the turbulence. It was then that my kayak rolled up on its left side putting my body practically parallel with the river's surface. Call it instinct, luck, or as I prefer, God's intervention, my paddle slapped flat and hard against the water as I snapped my torso to the right. It was a save! I had used this maneuver only one other time in the thousands of miles I have kayaked, and that was a few days before while going over a small water fall.

An eddy on river-right was a perfect spot to wait for Ed and a place for me to catch my breath. There was no way for him to know if I was in trouble halfway down the chute or if I was safely at the bottom. Later, he said he remained at the top for a few minutes before giving up a big *Geronimo shout.* Then he gave it his all.

Ed shot out the bottom of the chute like he was a member of the Jamaican bobsled team.

"Portage chute?! Why would anyone want to portage that?"

"Yeah!"

The trip through the effects of the upper chute was slightly more than a mile with a little taste of a Class IV at the very top, but the ride wasn't over. The river flowed through what seemed to be continuous Class I to Class II-plus rapids for eight more miles. Then we had a short intermission before hitting the Kilnabad Rapids, three more miles of Class I up and Class II. After this we had deeper water and good current with some sets of short rapids over gravel and rocky bands across the river.

It was an incredible day on the river. As an added bonus, the afternoon temps again reached into the seventies. Then the steep banks got us thinking about where we were going to camp.

As the day wore on, the limestone cliffs were replaced with lower bluffs and soft shoreline. It became more apparent that a decent campsite for the night may not be in the cards. This was the twenty-ninth day of our thirty-one day kayak trip, and a good day in spite of the shallow waters. The rapids and the challenge of Portage Chute made the dragging through the shallows worth it. According to the GPS, the river elevation dropped a little more than two hundred feet from where we had camped last night. The elevation change gave us everything from Class I to Class IV, all doable, no portages!

By the time "normal" folks would have called it a day, we had logged in forty miles and still were not ready to give up. It had been two hours since the last time we had to exit due to shallow waters. We were now less than sixty crow-fly miles from Hudson Bay, well within polar bear country. As the river made a wide sweep to the right we were presented with what Ed defined as the ideal site. There on river-left was a flat gravel wash over a small peninsula, seasoned with more than enough driftwood for a warm fire.

Ed asked what I thought. I checked the GPS for the time; 8:45 p.m., more two hours before the sun would disappear. Though it was tempting, early on in the day, Ed and I had agreed to take the first campsite <u>after</u> nine.

"We found one campsite, we'll find another. If the river continues to cooperate we can get a few more miles in." We paddled on, keeping one eye on the clock.

As the digits on the GPS flipped over to the top of the hour, I told Ed it was now time to begin the search for a place to set up our tents. We were both tired, but I was not overly eager to call it a day, clouds of blood-thirsty mosquitoes fogged the view of the shoreline. To make matters worse, I had promised to cook pancakes for tonight's dinner, with enough leftovers for a meal in the morning. The image of swatting while squatting over Ed's Coleman stove was not very pleasing to the mind's eye.

Immediately as I said it was nine o'clock, Ed exclaimed, "Is that a cabin up there?"

"Everything comes to you at the right moment. Be patient."
Unknown

It certainly was a cabin! We beached the kayaks on a boot-sucking mud flat and dragged them to somewhat drier ground, at least thirty feet from the river's edge. The first order of business was to throw on our rain coats and head nets. Then we needed to find out what accommodations, if any, awaited us up above. Our gear stayed behind for now while we went to explore the options. The thirty-foot-high climb would certainly have been less demanding had there been anything at all resembling a trail. Like most cabins you find in the wilderness, the door had a hasp for a padlock, but the only security was a small pin of some sort – no key required. I heard a long time ago cabin owners found that by leaving the place unlocked, it reduced the risk of vandalism. It's basically an open invitation, "Come in, make yourself at home, and leave everything exactly as you found it."

This cabin owner was more worried about a different type of vandal; bears. Outside the main entrance and beneath each window were unwelcome mats. There was also a second tier of bear deterrent. A solar panel atop a tall wooden pole was connected to deep cycle batteries providing juice for the electric fence that was attached to insulated stand-offs to the cabin's siding. There was no razor wire that we could see, but that's not to say it had not been a consideration, or perhaps was on the list of future upgrades. I doubt this cabin owner got his landscaping ideas from the same magazine I had for my home, then again, he probably wasn't going for curb appeal. There weren't any roads for who knows how many miles.

Inside the two-room cabin were enough bunks to sleep a half-dozen guests, a small Franklin stove (which fired up quickly), and shelves stocked with canned goods, snacks, and paper products. An assortment of guns: shotguns and deer rifles, or perhaps, bear rifles, hung on the wall. Fishing rods were standing in the corner with a couple of well supplied tackle boxes nearby, all set to go. Plates, silverware, glasses, cooking utensils, and an LP gas stove; who could ask for anything more? The place appeared to be meticulously clean and certainly well maintained. Our guess was that it belonged to someone who was most likely a pilot due to the amount of airplane paraphernalia decorating the interior.

The cabin option beat the heck out of setting up tents and going hand-to-hand combat with a few million mosquitoes on a muddy beach. However, the mosquitoes did motivate us to get our gear unloaded from the hatches and up the hillside without any unnecessary chitchat. To safeguard the kayaks for the night, I sprayed the hulls with DEET-based mosquito repellent. Ed thought it to be a waste of perfectly good bug repellent. I figured if it works on the little pests, it may work on the big ones too or at least enough to idle a bear's curiosity.

With a fire in the stove and bunks assigned, I began to make pancakes. As each pancake left the pan, I offered up a prayer of thanksgiving. Thanking God that I was not hunched up over a Coleman holding a spatula in one hand and swiping at the mosquitoes with the other, hoping not to get confused as to which hand would do the flipping and which hand would do the swiping. Total number of pancakes – three dozen, both dinner and breakfast taken care of!

When we declared *lights out* at midnight, the concern was oversleeping in the morning, so we set an alarm for 4:30. There was no way of knowing what was ahead or how fast we would be able to travel. We certainly did not want to linger too long in polar bear territory. It was the first time we used an alarm on the entire trip.

We left a thank-you note for our hosts and twenty dollars on the kitchen table before "checking out." Down on the mud beach we were glad to see that the bug spray worked! Our only means of transportation out of here had been spared from an assault by any nosy critters. We pushed off into the Churchill River with our stocking caps, or as they would say up here, "our tuques" pulled down tight over our ears to defend against the bite of the nippiness. The new day's sun painted a tinge of pink in the clear sky as it prepared to burn off the foggy haze hanging over the river.

Less than a mile downstream, we stopped paddling to drift in silence while a young bull moose supported on long lanky legs, waded awkwardly out from shore without any regard to our being there. He continued till only his head was above the surface. The gangly creature probably had only two things on his mind. One was a breakfast of whatever plant life that may be available on the river bottom. And two was to find refuge from mosquitoes, most likely both were of equal priority. The presence of two kayakers ten yards away seemed to be of no consequence.

Another mile and a half downstream, on the same shoreline that we had seen the moose, a lone timber wolf stood at water's edge. He gave us a cursory review before meandering off up and over the bank in the opposite direction of the moose. The river picked up a little speed after our sighting of the wolf, but the same conditions existed as the day before. Obviously the diversion dam hundreds of miles upstream from our position was open, sending up to eighty percent of the Churchill down to the Nelson. In spite of the low water level and having to traverse across from one side of the hundred-foot-wide river to the other to stay in the main flow, we were satisfied with the time we were making. We logged in twenty-one miles before our midday stop on a long gravel beach. It was the perfect invitation for a lunch break and opportunity to do my laundry.

The next major set of rapids labeled on the map was the Red Head, which we thought was a little disappointing, maybe a Class II. The topo map did not indicate any more rapids for the rest of the trip. However, around the next twist in the flow, we found the jackpot! It began with a Class I set of rapids, and over the next fifteen miles, the river flowed through a massive run of rocks and boulders yielding everything up to a solid Class III. Then the flow made a sharp bend to the left, across the wide open bed to where it narrowed to less than twenty feet wide. There it gained more velocity as it flowed violently between the two sheer walls of limestone over a perfectly flat rock, perhaps sixteen feet wide, right into an incredible standing wave that was well over our heads.

Interestingly, we didn't even stop to talk about options, nor did we give any thought to whether or not there was any structure hiding behind the wave. We just shot through! I was out front and Ed was directly behind me. It was a great culmination to all the rapids over the past month. On the other side, we briefly discussed whether we should empty our boats, circle around and do it again. It was determined that once was more than enough.

The river slowed, the wind picked up a bit, and life on the river was much more placid. At least until when I unintentionally came too close to four arctic terns who took great offense to my being where I was. For whatever reason, they became quite frantic. Immediately the alarm went out, sending them into their battle positions, diving at me from every direction in a coordinated assault that would have made any air force commander proud. As they kept coming in, one bomb run after another, I thrust my paddle at them and shouted, "I have a gun and I'm not afraid to use it!" As I reached for my shotgun, thinking the least I can do is make some noise to scare them away, the distance between whatever they were protecting and me was enough for them to call off the assault.

As I stated earlier, we didn't want to bring guns with us on this trip, but this is bear country – polar bear country! One source stated that contrary to popular belief, polar bears are not "man-eaters." That is, man is not their favorite food, and in all likelihood a healthy polar bear that is not starving will not normally go out of its way to catch and kill a human. In another source I read they are carnivores, and if a human is in their territory when they are hungry and hunting for a meal, the polar bear is very likely to treat the human as any other food source, killing it and eating it. And yet they, whoever they are, still say that polar bears are not man-eaters. Our guns have been "bear ready" for the past two days just to be on the safe side.

Polar bears weren't the only carnivores we were concerned about. We also read that polar bears have begun to breed with grizzly bears. There have been several cases in recent years where *grolar bears* (occasionally called *pizzly bears*) have been seen in the wild. The grolar bear is a relatively recent find, only proven to exist in the wild in 2006, when one was shot by an Idahoan hunter in Northern Canada. The jury is still out as to how this came about. The two species do not normally intermingle, for all I know it could simply be a case of "all the girls get prettier at closing time."

Ed was a touch more concerned about the big white Ursus maritimus than I, perhaps because he had spotted two in the past forty-eight hours. Both sightings ended with us breathing a heavy sigh of relief, after a long and indomitable observation of the creatures, when it became apparent the animals were not moving. And upon closer inspection they actually resembled rocks much more so than fierce bears. Nonetheless, Ed insisted that we make every effort to: a) not do any more night paddling, b) get close enough to the city of Churchill on our last full day so we could arrive midday and avoid being out at dusk or later, and c) take turns standing guard the last night to prevent being attacked while we slept in our tents. I thought (a) and (b) made good sense, but I wasn't about to agree to lose sleep over a potential polar bear attack.

Around seven o'clock we had passed through an area designated as Long Islands, a cluster of one large island and two smaller ones that stretched over six miles. Once past, the river widened to well over two and a half miles. Any evidence of the channel was gone and we were suddenly in a boulder field as far as we could see. Ed took the lead slogging out a trail, often wading in water waist-deep in pools too small to paddle. We had no choice but to go on. The conditions were absolutely dreadful.

Our feet, inside boots filled with bitter cold water, constantly searched to find the next foothold on the river bottom as we dragged our kayaks over the rocks. There were short distances of just small rocks like beach balls stuck in the river bottom. And there were patches of much larger boulders requiring actual climbing to get over them because they were too close together to get around.

When we could get back in our boats to paddle a hundred yards or so, our water-filled boots emptied into the cockpits, directly onto the seat. We continued in this debacle for nearly four hours. Then we found a channel deep enough and long enough to resume paddling, though yet scraping bottom occasionally.

A few minutes prior to midnight, when it became too dark to see what was out ahead, we could hear a set of rapids off to our right. This was the last night of our Churchill adventure and we were stuck in the middle of a river, at least a mile from either shore. Even if we could get to dry land, we had no guarantee we would find a place to pitch our tents. Paddling all night was certainly not an option either, not if there was a chance of encountering more of the same struggle we had been in earlier. The only choice remaining was to sleep in the kayaks. (To be honest, I've wanted to do this for a long time.)

A spattering of rocks the size of Georgian watermelons poking above the midstream shallows spread over fifteen feet or so became our campsite. We wedged the kayaks into the rocks on the upstream side. Next on the agenda: food, something hot, freeze-dried noodles and whatever else was in the package. It had been twelve hours since we had eaten anything. During that same twelve hours, Ed and I had easily burned a few thousand calories. Moving around our "campsite" while balancing precariously on the rocks in the darkness took time, making sure your feet were planted securely before leaning over or stretching to pick up something. We did not need to slip and get injured this late in the game. It took well over an hour to finish dinner, a process that in normal conditions would have been completed in a fraction of that time.

Then it was time to get ready for the night in the cockpit. Another ordeal in itself. Both of us had been in and out of the water all day, of course wet to the bone. It felt like the temperature had dropped at least thirty degrees, if not more, since we had begun our hike five hours earlier. The blessing was that there was no wind! I had a set of medium-weight long underwear that I had been using on the trip as pajamas. Those went on under my Farmer John wetsuit and my wet suit jacket. Pants and rain pants went on the bottom, and an extra shirt and paddling jacket on top. I also had a fresh pair of liner socks, a pair of *smart-wool* socks, and toe warmers that I had kept in reserve for just such an occasion. Confident this was indeed our last night I was willing to deploy all emergency gear.

I settled down in the cockpit with my neoprene spray skirt snapped tightly around the cowling to keep whatever heat I did produce inside the hull. My tuque was pulled down to meet the polar fleece gator around my neck that covered most of my face. Though I doubted I would need my PFD to keep me afloat, the extra layer of insulation felt good and the front provided a place to rest my chin. Finally a set of hand warmers were placed inside my choppers for the finishing touch. I was bundled up like a small child dressed by his mom to go out to play in the dead of winter. It was 2:30 a.m., but I could not resist as I looked over at Ed three feet away who was equally prepared, "Well Ed, it looks like you don't have to worry about being attacked by a polar bear in *your tent* tonight." With that being said I shut my eyes and drifted off into a deep sleep, knowing that it wasn't going to be me standing guard for rest of the night.

"Nothing shows a man's character more than
what he laughs at."
Clive James, Author

Our last "campsite" on the Churchill.

Sleeping in the kayaks had some distinct advantages, no gear to pack, and no tent to take down, though it was a very short night with no apparent need for an alarm clock. We began our last day as soon as there was enough light, simply pushing off the rocks into water deep enough to paddle. Paddling lasted no longer than ten minutes. The rapids we had heard in the dark were not much more than some riffles. The riffles turned first into deeper waters then, just as quickly, that deep water flowed through another boulder field. Our hiking, wading, and intermittent paddling lasted nearly three hours, but we made it seven miles closer to our destination in those three hours. In and out of our kayaks a dozen times or more, wading chest-deep in pools of cold dark water less than thirty feet across, then up over huge rocks the size of refrigerators. Do I need to mention how cold the water was? At least I was wearing my wet suit.

We had only fifteen more miles to go before reaching our destination on Hudson Bay. The worst was behind us as we entered a pool area created by a weir Manitoba Hydro had built six miles downstream from the town of Churchill. The intent of the rock weir was to enhance water levels on the Churchill River, thirty years after the diversion project. Engineers projected an increased river depth of approximately six feet for a distance of approximately seven miles upstream from the weir. This depth would diminish further upstream. We were now reaping the benefits of the weir! The weir was designed to re-water a portion of the Churchill River that had been dewatered since the completion of the Churchill River Diversion project. Approximately 1,200 acres of former riverbed was to be re-watered, and approximately 420 acres of additional land would be flooded.

When Ed and I finally reached the weir, it was much larger than we had imagined. Obviously, we hadn't put much thought into it. The river was well over a mile wide at this point and the weir crossed the river at an angle. The last thing we wanted to do was to have to climb over the top of it. Not that it was that high, but it appeared that only the sharpest of rocks were recruited for the project.

We followed a small flow through a backwater on the upstream side to where we found a boat landing. More reconnaissance gave way to a relatively easy re-entry point. Six miles remaining and closing fast! Somewhere around the three-mile mark, we reached the "salt line" where the freshwater river met the salt water from Hudson Bay. The temperature inside the cockpits dropped dramatically. I checked the water temperature, 36F! It was July 1.

My wife, Sharron, and our friends, Cliff and Lois, left home three days ago. Cliff and Lois have been our close friends for many years, always willing to lend a hand, and always willing to go on an adventure. They had driven the six hours to Winnipeg where they stayed over and got on the train to Churchill the next morning. The two day train ride had recently been featured on the History channel as the sixteenth of the top twenty most scenic rail excursions in the world. If all had gone well, they were to arrive the very morning that Ed and I were too. Because Sharron had been traveling the past three days, I had not been in contact with her by satellite phone. But nevertheless, I had a vision of how our arrival was going to go. Their train should have arrived around 7:00 a.m. and our ETA was noon. As we were making our final approach, counting down the remaining miles, I shared my thoughts with Ed. "I couldn't find any photos of the harbor in Churchill, but the way I see it, there will be some sort of low sea wall along a walkway near the water. It's concrete with an iron railing. When we get about a half mile away, Sharron, Cliff and Lois will just be walking up to the railing. They'll look out, see us coming and start jumping up and down, waving, and hugging one another. It's going to be awesome!"

The frigid waters didn't hamper our efforts. The only thing that would slow us down now was possibly a sighting of beluga whales. In summertime, the Hudson Bay and Churchill River are alive with beluga whales. They are friendly and curious and have even been known to allow people to swim among them, so why wouldn't they like to have a couple of kayaks in their midst? Two miles to go, a mile to go, a half-mile to go, and no concrete sea wall, no railing, and no friendly faces there to cheer us to the finish line. There was however, a pickup truck pulling up to the boat landing, a brand new white Ford F-150 with a half dozen brightly colored helium balloons tied off to both side mirrors. "There they are!!!" And then, the pickup drove away. It didn't even stop. But we made it! As anti-climatic as it was at the time, we made it; 1,220 miles over thirty days, twenty-five portages not counting the train from Thicket Portage and the airplane from Thompson.

Another truck with a boat trailer hanging on behind it approached the landing within minutes of our arrival. Exactly as it had been all along our entire journey, what we needed was there when we needed it. The two fishermen were gracious enough to delay their outing long enough to help us get our boats and gear to the railroad depot.

There we connected with folks who were more than helpful in getting everything stored away in a safe location.

Next stop was the hotel to see if Sharron and our friends made it. They were sitting in the lobby worrying about us when we showed up, to put an end to that nonsense! Hugs, hugs, and more hugs, dampened with a few tears of joy. As soon as we could, we asked about all the brouhaha that was going on in town. It looked like a big celebration, and believe it or not, by now we figured out it wasn't for us!

It was of course, July 1, Canada Day. Canada Day is the national day of Canada, a federal statutory holiday celebrating the anniversary of the July 1, 1867 enactment of the British North America Act, 1867, which united three colonies into a single country called Canada within the British Empire.

So what if the celebration wasn't in any way related to our success, that didn't mean that we couldn't partake in some of the festivities – after a very long, hot shower of course.

In the park, the city was having a free BBQ. Sharron didn't hesitate to introduce Ed and me to the others we had joined at one of the picnic tables, telling them what we had just completed. It sparked a great deal of interest! People thought we were crazy. One fellow asked, "What did you do at Portage Chute?"

"Ran it."

"You guys are nuts! There's a lot of guns and fishing gear at the bottom of that one," he said.

The parade "in our honor."

Our arrival.

The kayaks loaded in a boxcar headed for home.

Without a doubt, people who live in Churchill are some of the highest quality you could find anywhere in the world. I doubt we met each one of the eight hundred residents, but it certainly felt like it. We spent the next two days exploring Churchill, including a boat trip back out into the bay we had paddled through to observe a pod of belugas that we had missed by less than a hundred yards on our way in. Our tourist itinerary of the city also included a trip to Fort Churchill, located five miles east of the town.

The fort has a great history… Europeans first arrived in the area in 1619 led by Jens Munk. The exploration wintered where Churchill would later stand. Only three of sixty-four expedition members survived that winter. The following spring, they sailed one of the expedition's two ships back to Denmark. In 1717 the Hudson's Bay Company built a log fort a few miles upstream from the mouth of the Churchill River, the first permanent settlement. Between 1731-1741, the log fort was replaced with Prince of Wales Fort which was built of stone. In 1782 the French made an unsuccessful attempt to demolish the fort. The worst effect was on the natives, who had become dependent on trade goods from the fort, and many of them starved. In 1783, the English returned to build a new fort, a short distance upriver. Due to its proximity from areas of heavy competition between the North West Company and the Hudson's Bay Company, it remained a stable, if not profitable, source of furs.

As fur trading began to decline while western agriculture became more successful, Churchill's economy suffered greatly. After decades of bitter politics regarding the domination of the Canadian Pacific Railway, western Canadian governments consolidated their efforts and lobbied for the creation of a major shipping harbor on Hudson Bay, connected by rail from Winnipeg. (Initially the route was to Port Nelson, but after years of effort and millions of dollars, this project was abandoned and Churchill was chosen as the alternative after World War I.) Construction of the railroad was extremely slow and the rail line itself did not come to Churchill until 1929. It was another three years before commercial shipping of agricultural products became viable. At that same time, the railroad began to take on passengers. In 1942, the United States Army Air Corps established a base at Churchill. After World War II, the base was jointly operated by Canada and the United States for training purposes and continued to operate until the mid-1960s. There are no roads leading to Churchill. Aside from the railroad, Churchill is serviced by two scheduled airlines offering flights to and from Winnipeg and to points north of Churchill in Nunavut, the largest, northernmost territory of Canada. The airport is also part of the former Fort Churchill military base and has a runway large enough to land the space shuttle.

While we were at the fort, park rangers armed with 12 gauge shotguns patrolled the perimeter on ATVs on the lookout for polar bears. There had been a sighting of a polar bear the day after we arrived, but no shots were fired. I asked one of the rangers if they used progressive loads; first shot being a light load, primarily for making noise; the second load being buck shot; and the third load, a solid slug. "Nope, just slugs. If a bear gets too close to our visitors, we don't give it a second chance."

A visit to Churchill would not be complete without spending an hour or two touring the Eskimo Museum. Not a real exciting museum, but definitely interesting. On display is a stuffed polar bear and a musk ox, narwhal horns and original hide-covered kayaks, weaponry such as tiny arrowheads and big harpoon blades. Art work including hundreds of carvings portraying intricate scenes of everyday life fill the voids.

We explored, we rested, and we ate. Then we rested and ate some more. The train left for Winnipeg on the evening of our third day in Churchill, fifty-four hours after our arrival. The train provided yet another community and another adventure. Over the next two days we got to know our fellow passengers and I still connect with some on Facebook. When we arrived in Winnipeg, our gear was loaded onto Cliff's pickup and we headed for home to make sure Ed arrived in time to teach his summer class.

Though my Churchill adventure was by far the most demanding of all my adventures, physically and mentally, it was the most fulfilling, spiritually.

***"And He knows the number of hairs on your head!
Never fear, you are far more valuable to him
than a whole flock of sparrows."
Luke 12:7***

Not the best campsite, but it worked.

One of the boat ladders.

Twilight from an island.

Gear List for the Trip

The following is a fairly comprehensive list of equipment we took along on our trip. As with any outing or excursion it is the sole responsibility of each individual to determine what gear is actually required for a safe and successful adventure.

Paddling…

- Boat
- Paddle, Cruising
- Paddle, River
- Paddle Float
- Life Jacket
- Reflective Safety Vest (for big water and night paddling)
- Seat Cushion
- Heal Cushion
- Deck Bag
- Maps (2 copies)
- Waterproof Map Case
- GPS
- Compass
- Charging Unit and/or Spare Batteries
- Pre-paid Phone Card
- Satellite Phone with Extra Battery (rented)
- SPOT Personal Locator
- Sunglasses

Camping

- Tent
- Sleeping Pad
- Sleeping Bag (20 degree minimum)
- Emergency Space Blanket
- Pillow (if desired)
- Tent Patch Kit
- Sleeping Pad Patch Kit
- Ear Plugs
- Wet Wipes (large)
- Water Filter
- Water Purification Tablets

Crystal Lite (or similar product)
PowerAde (or similar sports drink)
Nalgene Bottles (4)
Camera
Camp Stool
Go-Jo Type Hand Cleaner
Biodegradable Hand Soap
Biodegradable Laundry Soap
Hand Sanitizer
Microfiber Camp Towel
Portable Urinal
Toilet Tissue
Duffle / Portage Bag
Portaging Straps
Wind Proof Lighter
Striker
Matches (in waterproof container)
Set Wood Fire Starters
Folding Saw
Multi Tool
Sheath Knife
Knife Sharpener (small wet stone)
Headlamp (2)
Flashlight
Large Trash Bag
Small Trash Bags
Paper Towel
Rollup Cutting Board
Fishing Rod
Fishing Tackle
Fillet Knife
Parachute Cord (200 feet, 550 lb)
Weapon (12 gauge with slugs or 30.06 minimum)
Weapons Permits
Ammunition

Clothes
Wet Suit
Waterproof Boots (Neoprene)

Neoprene Socks
Camp Shoes
Socks, (3 pair, smartwool)
Socks, (3 pair, disposable)
Briefs, (6 pair, disposable)
Quick Dry Zip-off Pants
Tee Shirt
Insulated Underwear Bottoms (light weight)
Insulated Underwear Top (light weight)
Insulated Underwear Bottoms (medium weight)
Insulated Underwear Top (medium weight)
Wind Pants
Wind Breaker Jacket
Rain Pants
Paddling Jacket (waterproof)
Wide Brim Hat
Polar Fleece Hat & Neck Gator
Paddling Gloves
Leather Gloves
Neoprene Gloves
Mosquito Net (2)
Laundry Bag

Cooking
Lightweight Camp Stove, ex Jet Boil
Extra Fuel Canisters (3)
Alcohol Wipes
Cooking Oil
Fry Pan (small one-egg type)
Insulated Cup
Plate or Bowl (3 cup covered container)
Spoon
Small Spatula
Toothpicks
Seasoning and Hot Sauce

Food Suggestions
Bagels
Tortillas

Ramen Noodles
Instant Potatoes (Idaho brand)
Gravy Mix
Stove Top Dressing
Knorr Sides
Mountain House Meals
Foil Packed Chicken
Foil Packed Sandwich-ready Tuna Spread
Pancake Mix
Peanut Butter
Nutritional / Protein Bars
Sweet & Salty Nut Bars
Snack Bars
Dry Roasted Peanuts
Trail Mix
Red Licorice

Safety
Personal Toiletries
Spare Set of Eyeglasses (if necessary)
Ace Bandage
Band Aids
Surgical Tape
Tendonitis Sleeve(s)
Bandanas (3)
Super Glue
Benadryl
Sun Screen
Burn Gel (topical cooling gel contains Lidocaine)
Hand Lotion (for cracked skin)
Lip Balm
Vasoline
Baby Powder
Disinfectant
Neosporin
Ibuprofen
Ibuprofen PM
Imodium AD
General Antibiotic (filled Rx from your Dr.)

Dental Floss
Magnifying Glass
Fingernail Clipper
Tick Removal Device
Hand / Foot Warmers
Inspect Repellent (plus extra)

Other
Bible / Other Reading Material
Passport
Waterproof Notebook & Pencil
Duct Tape
Plastic Wire Ties (various sizes)
Carabiners (6 +/-)
Spare Screws and Nuts (for the kayak)
Weather Radio
Wrist Watch
MP3 Player

GPS Coordinates Along the Route

Log into Googlemaps.com for satellite imaging.

Minnesota...

N47 14.168 W93 31.684	Grand Rapids, MN
N47 29.916 W93 54.086	Bowstring Lake Public Access
N47 35.474 W94 00.710	Sand Lake
N47 38.813 W94 01.776	Little Sand Lake
N47 39.897 W94 02.692	Rice Lake
N47 44.387 W94 03.067	Dora Lake Access
N47 45.387 W94 02.488	Big Fork River
N47 45.512 W93 52.763	Robs Rapids, Big Fork River
N47 45.749 W93 49.261	Hauck Rapids, Big Fork River
N47 44.829 W93 39.164	Big Fork, MN
N47 50.424 W93 30.196	MN Hwy 1 Bridge
N47 52.629 W93 35.778	Muldoon Rapids, Big Fork River
N47 55.235 W93 37.292	Little American Falls, Big Fork River
N47 57.017 W93 42.174	Powells Rapids, Big Fork River
N48 11.463 W93 48.160	Big Falls, MN
N48 31.010 W93 43.004	Rainy River
N48 50.367 W94 41.594	Wheelers Pt, MN (Lake of the Woods)

Lake of the Woods to the Bloodvein River...

N48 57.345 W94 32.508	Harris Hill Resort, Lake of the Woods
N49 45.875 W94 29.555	Marina in Kenora, Ontario
N49 45.875 W94 33.420	Portage Bay
N49 52.428 W94 33.308	Winnipeg River, Ontario
N49 55.000 W94 32.901	Winnipeg River, Ontario
N50 04.577 W94 44.296	Winnipeg River, Ontario
N50 07.198 W94 48.541	Winnipeg River, Ontario
N50 06.892 W94 52.040	Whitedog Falls Hydro Plant
N50 11.467 W95 04.203	Winnipeg River, Ontario
N50 15.572 W95 09.745	Winnipeg River, Ontario
N50 20.127 W95 12.936	Winnipeg River, Ontario

N50 22.299 W95 24.140 Halliday Rapids, Winnipeg River
N50 20.196 W95 29.724 Winnipeg River, Manitoba
N50 18.407 W95 32.342 Pointe du Bois Hydro Plant

N50 13.470 W95 33.754 Slave Falls Hydro Plant
N50 11.011 W95 37.250 Scots Rapids
N50 09.382 W95 39.168 Sturgeon Falls
N50 09.427 W95 51.955 Pinawa, Manitoba
N50 07.127 W96 00.955 Seven Sisters Hydro Plant
N50 23.647 W95 59.850 MacAurthor Falls Hydro Plant
N50 27.724 W96 00.508 Great Falls Hydro Plant
N50 34.113 W96 10.558 Pine Falls Hydro Plant
N50 43.913 W96 22.956 Travers Bay on Lake Winnipeg

Lake Winnipeg, Lower Basin

N50 57.113 W96 23.148 Lil Birch Point
N51 04.452 W96 26.722 Observation Point
N51 09.352 W96 24.528 Ciermer's Point
N51 39.343 W96 41.356 The Narrows

Lake Winnipeg, Upper Basin

N51 45.690 W96 48.907 Princess Harbour, Bloodvein River

Bloodvein River to Cross Lake…

N51 52.049 W96 53.123 Lake Winnipeg, Upper Basin
N51 59.514 W96 52.787 Split Rock Point
N52 01.851 W96 55.109 Whoopee Harbour
N52 03.926 W96 58.827 Lake Winnipeg, Upper Basin
N52 06.406 W96 59.607 Lake Winnipeg, Upper Basin
N52 09.399 W97 03.165 Lake Winnipeg, Upper Basin
N52 14.636 W97 07.242 Lake Winnipeg, Upper Basin
N52 19.308 W97 05.622 Lake Winnipeg, Upper Basin
N52 23.758 W97 08.080 Lake Winnipeg, Upper Basin
N52 32.518 W97 09.968 Lake Winnipeg, Upper Basin
N52 37.717 W97 13.138 Lake Winnipeg, Upper Basin
N52 45.444 W97 20.422 Lake Winnipeg, Upper Basin
N52 51.364 W97 24.679 Lake Winnipeg, Upper Basin
N52 57.518 W97 27.916 Lake Winnipeg, Upper Basin

N53 03.862 W97 25.956	Lake Winnipeg, Upper Basin
N53 10.151 W97 26.396	Lake Winnipeg, Upper Basin
N53 18.558 W97 35.706	Lake Winnipeg, Upper Basin
N53 24.886 W97 40.877	Lake Winnipeg, Upper Basin
N53 29.399 W97 42.761	Lake Winnipeg, Upper Basin
N53 36.503 W97 50.175	Lake Winnipeg, Upper Basin
N53 42.064 W97 49.106	Entering Playgreen Lake
N53 54.831 W97 58.993	Leaving Playgreen Lake
N53 59.017 W97 50.121	Norway House, Manitoba
N54 03.375 W97 44.498	Nelson River, Manitoba
N54 06.468 W97 42.920	Nelson River, Manitoba
N54 08.693 W97 40.955	Nelson River, Manitoba
N54 11.886 W97 37.989	Nelson River, Manitoba
N54 13.466 W97 37.370	Nelson River, Manitoba
N54 15.523 W97 33.882	Nelson River, Manitoba
N54 17.804 W97 32.774	Nelson River, Manitoba
N54 19.833 W97 35.479	Nelson River, Manitoba
N54 21.508 W97 35.883	Nelson River, Manitoba
N54 27.155 W97 37.509	Nelson River, Manitoba
N54 28.425 W97 37.047	Nelson River, Manitoba
N54 31.338 W97 38.722	Pipestone Lake, Manitoba
N54 33.478 W97 43.629	Nelson River, Manitoba
N54 36.119 W97 46.666	Nelson River, Manitoba
N54 37.426 W97 47.010	Cross Lake, Manitoba

Cross Lake to the Churchill River…

N54 42.326 W97 52.910	Planned Exit to Nelson (canceled when we heard the falls)
N54 42.326 W97 47.410	Alternative Exit to Nelson
N54 44.748 W97 51.481	Nelson River, Manitoba
N54 48.107 W98 01.049	Nelson River, Manitoba
N54 51.840 W98 01.250	Nelson River, Manitoba
N54 54.086 W98 01.131	Nelson River, Manitoba
N54 56.805 W97 54.930	Entering Sipiwesk Lake
N54 59.534 W97 42.671	Sipiwesk Lake
N55 02.028 W97 34.527	Sipiwesk Lake
N55 03.874 W97 31.212	Sipiwesk Lake

N55 06.063 W97 29.390	Sipiwesk Lake
N55 08.350 W97 23.955	Sipiwesk Lake
N55 11.155 W97 21.712	Sipiwesk Lake
N55 13.470 W97 18.872	Portage to Sabomin Lake
N55 15.325 W97 19.641	Leaving Sabomin Lake
N55 15.792 W97 19.868	Entry to Landing Lake
N55 18.524 W97 40.310	Boat Landing at Thicket Portage
N55 44.352 W97 52.019	Thompson, Manitoba
N56 31.680 W97 14.999	Campbell Lake
N56 30.434 W96 58.049	Pelletier Lake
N56 35.282 W96 20.196	Wasaiowaka Lake
N56 34.686 W96 14.955	Donlop's Fly-In Lodge & Outposts
N56 35.079 W96 15.655	Little Churchill River
N56 39.601 W96 06.859	Little Churchill River
N56 41.788 W96 01.315	Little Churchill River
N56 42.061 W96 00.573	Little Churchill River
N56 50.190 W95 47.142	Little Churchill River
N56 56.930 W95 45.245	Lodge on Recluse Lake
N56 56.254 W95 41.319	Little Churchill River
N57 02.305 W95 36.703	Little Churchill River
N57 06.568 W95 34.295	Little Churchill River
N57 21.898 W95 21.300	Little Churchill River
N57 30.604 W95 21.454	Confluence with the Churchill River

Churchill River to Churchill...

N57 34.252 W95 26.592	Churchill River
N57 39.203 W95 28.074	Churchill River
N57 40.673 W95 27.620	Churchill River
N58 20.012 W94 19.027	Churchill River
N58 29.933 W94 15.310	Churchill River
N58 40.454 W94 11.543	Weir on the Churchill River
N58 46.754 W94 11.743	Churchill, Manitoba

ISBN 9781439253106

How many times have you been trapped at work daydreaming of escaping from the ho-hum doldrums to an adventure of exploring the unknown, casting aside pleas from your mother to be careful and the need to focus on detail instilled by your father?

As we stood on the shore of Lake Itasca in northern Minnesota, ready to embark on an adventure of a lifetime, it had been only nine days since Luke and Andy entered my office to discuss an idea devised over lunch. "Let's paddle the entire Mississippi River from the Headwaters to the Gulf, BUT, not all in one trip. We can do one section at a time, as work schedules allow." In less time than it takes to finish a cup of coffee, the decision is made to go ahead even though not one of us has a clue as to the length of the Mississippi. With little thought to detailed planning, we strike out to conquer the third largest river in the world. The chronological travelogue covers the highlights as we paddle our way through uninhabited wilderness and along the banks of river towns. Well seasoned with a good measure of humor, the narrative blends stories of people, places, and history. Anyone interested in the outdoors and/or travel who enjoys the lighthearted approach will love this book. It goes beyond the 'how-to' of paddling and gets into the adventure itself. Ka-Ka-Ska-Ska is truly an inspiration to others to, "Just do it!"

Made in United States
Orlando, FL
26 April 2022